Empathy Stories: Heart, Connection, & Inspiration

Edited by Mary Goyer
With 30+ Empathy Contributors

© 2016

Empathy Stories: Heart, Connection, & Inspiration

First Printing, 2016

Conscious Communication
499 Via Casitas
Greenbrae, CA 94904
www.consciouscommunication.co

Table of Contents

Introduction 1

Empathy At Home: Connections With Loved Ones 5

My Teenager's Pain - Kristin Masters.................................... 5

New Year's Eve Argument - Mark Schneider........................ 8

Processing Alzheimer's - Mary Goyer 11

Sitting on Opposite Sides of the Couch - Jim Manske..........17

A Better Outcome - Sura Hart...22

Connecting With My Mom - LaShelle Lowe-Charde 24

A Father's Gift - Miki Kashtan 28

Kitty Empathy - Dian Killian 31

A Hit Instead of a Kiss - Mair Alight 35

Empathy Cards During An Argument - Becka Kelley............37

Blueberry Meltdown - Alan Seid...41

Overwhelmed Granny - Anne Walton.................................44

Hating School - Cedar Rose Selenite 47

Unsolicited Advice - Mark Schneider 50

A Time Out For Reflection - Mair Alight 55

Teenage Gratitude - Penny Wassman...................................58

Different Ways of Showing Love - Kristin Masters 61

Whining Kids - Sura Hart...64

Bike-Riding Mishap - Jean Morrison 66

The Little Lamb - Aya Caspi...68

Inner-Child Rescue - Sarah Peyton 75

Empathy at Work: Creating a Culture of Compassion 78

Misbehaving for the Substitute - Victoria Kindle Hodson... 78

One Versus the Committee - Kevin Goyer 84

Man to Man Empathy - Timothy Regan 88

Autonomy & Safety for Five-Year-Olds - Matthew Rich 93

A Dying Patient - Anne Walton 96

Hospital Execs - Jim Manske 98

"Master" Teacher - Mary Goyer.. 102

Disdain From My Research Supervisor - Hema Pokharna. 106

Saving Personnel During Budget Cuts - Dian Killian.......... 108

Apologizing to My Students - Kevin Goyer 112

Empathy in the Community: Caring for Strangers 115

Car, the Clubs, and the Cab Driver - Thom Bond 115

Heckling Baseball Fans - Becka Kelley 118

Furious Neighbours - Manuela Santiago-Teigeler 122

Intensity and Diversity - Timothy Regan 124

A Prisoner's Insight - Mair Alight 130

From Self-Loathing to Self-Acceptance in Ten Minutes -
Katherine Revoir.. 132

Zeke and the KKK - Catherine Cadden.............................. 137

Antidote to Road Rage - Mark Schultz 141

Surviving Gun Point - Srinath Waidler-Barker 143

Feeling Out of Place - Edwin Rutsch...................................149

Questioned by the Cops - Christine King...........................154

Jack's Funeral - Bridget Belgrave 156

Reframing the Unthinkable - Carol Chase 162

Left Behind - Jim Manske..164

Publishing Your Inspiring Empathy Story 169

Empathy Practitioners: Biographies..................................172

Appendix A: "Not Empathy" Quick Reference Sheet.........183

Appendix B: Planned Empathy Practice 185

Appendix C: Special Notes for Newbies 190

About the Editor...195

Introduction

Connection

My dad's side of the family has a particular penchant for storytelling—and zero qualms about exaggerating. *You've heard about the time when Grandma, as a young girl, was "running the traps" in the forest with urine in her canteen, right? Yeah. One day, she rode her horse to each of her family's animal traps, soaking them with pee to lure in new critters, when she was approached by some men who seemed to want a drink from her canteen. She was scared of the strangers and, since there was a language barrier, she didn't know what to do. She tried to gesture and grimace them into understanding that she had no water for them, repeating, "You don't want this!" But they kept pointing to the container, insisting. Finally, she threw the whole canteen towards them with a cringe, and galloped away as fast as she could.*

I have no idea how true this story is, but it doesn't entirely matter. Even tall tales help people bond and, in the case of my family get-togethers, we use them to remind ourselves of what we have in common. Stories help create a safe perimeter from politics, religion, and family dirt; retelling old stories helps us relax and set the stage for deeper dives of connection. *Did you hear about the time when Dad's mischievous uncles told Mom, his new bride, that if they were going to work on a shed for Great-Grandma's house, Mom would have to straighten out all the bent, rusty nails by hand?* Whether we're laughing about our uncles' pranks or daring to enter the riskier territory of our personal ups and downs, story-telling weaves an almost magic togetherness. Our differences effectively suspend themselves for a stretch of time and we find ourselves connecting, without even trying.

Learning and Growing

Connection is key, but we also *learn best through hearing stories*. Our brains need examples! When I was first introduced to Non-Violent Communication, the anecdotes I heard struck me the most. Marshall Rosenberg, the founder of NVC, often shared in his workshops a story about two warring village chiefs from Nigeria, who came together to meet with him after years of escalating violence and murder. Each blamed the other for the mounting bloodshed – a fairly common narrative in our world, wouldn't you say?

Using a relatively simple process, he helped shift the conversation between them quickly, enabling them to discover their commonalities.

During a single session, one of the chiefs said, "If we could talk like this with each other, then we wouldn't have to kill each other."

Within *just a few hours*, both chiefs went from threats and accusations to acknowledging their shared concerns for equality and safety. Soon after articulating these two needs, along with a few others, they came up with a peace resolution plan for their tribes. How did this happen after years had passed and countless lives had been lost? That is the magic of empathy!

Empathy Stories

A story can, indeed, be the catalyst for a powerful revolution. As you read the forty+ stories here, you'll encounter some new ways to talk to the people in your life. And as you revisit them, you'll notice new techniques you didn't even see at first glance—stories can be stealthy that way. In the end, my wish for you is that your life will be changed, in no uncertain terms, because you see how powerful it can be to lean in towards connection, one conversation at a time…

Visit www.consciouscommunication.co for
guides to:
Transforming Difficult Conversations
Starting Your Own Listening & Empathy Circle
Conscious Communication in the Classroom: Basic
Steps for Educators

Empathy At Home: Connections With Loved Ones

My Teenager's Pain - Kristin Masters

One of the frames I often use when teaching parenting classes is, *Where do you have a hard time with your kid having a hard time?*

This question came up for me in relation to my daughter, recently. I had just come home after working away for five days. My sixteen-year-old seemed to be in a bad mood, and I initially thought it was about me. But I made eye contact with her and watched her as she slumped down on the couch, saying, "Everything's bad."

I could feel the desire in me to come up to reassure her or talk her out of it, even though she hadn't mentioned any details, yet. Instead, I said gently, "Well, what is it? What do you want me to know?"

She hesitated, but as she began to deliver her story, I understood that she was feeling left out by some friends who were spending more time with each other than with her. There were so many times during this halted story delivery that I felt the impulse to jump in and tell her, "Oh, they totally adore you. They love you."

Or I could've given her advice like, "Well, you

know, have you asked them this? Have you asked them that?"

But I somehow managed to hold my tongue on unsolicited advice and unrequested reassurance. Instead, I stuck with the basics of reflection, empathy, and plain old listening.

One of the things I remember saying was, "So, when they go off at fourth period and spend time together you end up, sounds like, feeling lonely, you know? Is it that you wish they knew how much you miss them, but it feels a little bit too vulnerable, maybe, to say that?"

She softened and cried. She said, "Yeah, it's like I feel stuck. I can't really express anything to them. I can't say anything to them because they'd just blow it off."

What also came out as she talked was that she had tried to express her concern to several other friends, and all of them had basically either given her advice or reassurance, and she was so discouraged that they didn't really seem to hear her.

By the end of the twenty minutes that we sat together, she had both laughed and cried. She said she felt some relief, and thanked me for listening. I felt close to her and she felt heard. I really had this sense that I had averted a reinforcement of the "nobody listening" experience that she was getting from her friends.

On top of that, I realize that if I'd have moved forward with the assumption she was mad at me, I would have, perhaps, cut her off at the very beginning, which would've been such a missed opportunity to feel like I got to meet her in a place that we all experience: that sense of being left out, of wanting to know that we matter and belong, and that our friends adore us. I really would have missed something super sweet.

- Kristin Masters, www.nvcsantacruz.org

New Year's Eve Argument - Mark Schneider

One New Year's Eve, a few years back, I saw first-hand the simple yet almost miraculous transformative power of empathy. My wife and I had a quiet dinner with another couple, then came back to our house at around 9:00pm. We live close to our downtown area, where there is always a big festive partying atmosphere on New Year's, and we could hear the voices and shouts of people beginning to congregate.

We spent some time together, talking about the evening we'd enjoyed with our friends. After a while, my wife said that she was tired and ready for bed. I relaxed while she got ready for bed, still able to hear the sounds of revelers in the streets downtown.

As she pulled out a book and climbed into bed, I told her that I wanted to go check out the scene outside. I'm fairly extroverted, love being around lots of people, so walking around downtown seemed like the perfect thing to do. I could people-watch and perhaps run into friends. It certainly didn't make any sense to hang around the house, wide awake, if my wife was going to be asleep.

"Why do you always have to go out?" she asked, clearly annoyed. "Can't you ever just stay at home?"

I felt my whole body tense up because I love going out; I feel enlivened when I'm around people. My wife and I'd had a nice evening together. She was in bed, planning to be asleep soon. I couldn't see any reason why I should stay at home doing nothing.

A short pause gave me just enough time to wonder if there might be something else going on. It wasn't easy, though. Almost every fiber in my being interpreted her words as untrue (I don't always need to go out). And it registered, in the moment, as a full and total disaster for my prospects of living a happy life because I was married to a woman who was painfully judgmental of such an innocent, important thing for me.

All of this was boiling inside but, taking a deep breath, I still managed to ask, "Can you say more?"

She repeated, "You always need to go out. You just can't ever stay home."

Ugh. *Keep going. Don't give up, I told myself.*

"Can you tell me more about what's going on for you? What are you needing?" I asked.

She repeated herself again, and then said something new. "I'm not feeling well, and don't want to be alone. I want someone to be with me, and take care of me!"

"Oh!" That's what she was really asking for.

Even though I was still triggered by the conversation, when I heard what she wanted, I immediately recognized how much I wanted to give it to her. It superseded my desire to go downtown and be part of the festivities. So, I stayed home, a bit shaken, but happy to be able to show my love for her. Being able to translate her words made such a difference.

Processing Alzheimer's - Mary Goyer

With my partner still asleep beside me, I stayed in bed one morning, noticing I was in a funk. A dear friend had been in the hospital, and the trips back and forth to visit her were certainly a little hectic. But something else felt really off, and I was having trouble putting my finger on the pulse of it.

I kept thinking about my friend, Sherry, and how fast her life had gone from normal to complicated. A momentary slip on a wet driveway had led to her needing ankle surgery. The procedure went well and she'd been released from the hospital, yet her body required the support of a month-long stay at an inpatient rehab facility.

It was depressing and dingy, this rehab place, but her spirits remained quite high. Even though her injuries were purely physical, there were a lot of people there who had suffered from strokes, Alzheimer's, and other maladies affecting cognitive functioning. True to her personality, she took the whole experience on as an "opportunity" and began connecting with everyone she met, learning their stories.

Her attitude was inspiring to me, but I still didn't like that she was there. I began to cry, and hearing me, my partner woke up.

"Hey," he said, "What is it?"

"I'm overwhelmed thinking about this rehab place. The other night, when I was visiting, it was pretty shocking. Sherry seems to be keeping her chin up about being there. But it's disturbing. The hallways were dark. Her neighbor in the next room was screaming, 'Help me, they've kidnapped me!' throughout the entire time I was there, which is apparently a normal thing. And then a call button alarm at the nurse's station rang for a half-hour straight. I went up and said something to the person behind the counter about the alarm and she replied back to me, 'Yeah, I've gotten used to the sound so I don't even notice it anymore.' I was appalled. 'Doesn't it mean someone needs something, though?' I asked her."

"Wow," he replied, pulling me into a hug. "That's unsettling."

"And I just can't stop thinking about my dad ending up in one of those places, with people behind the counter ignoring alerts. I mean, I had to tell myself that they must be ignoring it for a reason, since the lady was so nonchalant when I asked her about it, but it was hard to listen to for so long. I could hear it all the way in Sherry's room!"

"So this takes you to your dad, huh? You're thinking about him in that kind of environment?"

"Yes! It's horrifying!"

The tears really started coming down. My dad had been diagnosed with Alzheimer's that previous year, and it was disheartening visiting this place which foreshadowed a potential future for him.

"I mean, I know we're not there, yet. And it could be ten more years before we are. But there's possibly going to come a time when he's going to need more care than we can give him at home…" I trailed off.

"And you're worried about how that's going to be?" he asked.

"Yes." My mind was all over the place. "But I can't even say 'we.' I don't feel like I'm doing enough now, honestly. Stephen and Kathy are taking on the bulk of things, aside from my mom. I'd told myself I'd fly into town every few months to lend a hand – or at least for the sake of a visit – and I haven't. I've only gone twice. It seems so insufficient."

"Feeling guilty? You want to help out more?"

"Yeah. It's hard. I was hoping Kevin would make a trip out to help this summer. He and I talked about it several times but it never happened. And then I never went, either. I really want to be there while my dad is still himself so we can connect, you know? We have no idea how long we're going to get. I mean, we talk on the phone all the time, but... I don't know."

"So," he reflected, "some of this is about you and your brother helping out Stephen, Kathy, and your mom back home, everyone working together. And some of it is just about valuing the time you have left with your dad?"

"Exactly!" I paused for a bit, switching gears. "It's making me think of this Alzheimer's patient I met at the rehab place while eating with Sherry in the TV room. I was working on a jigsaw puzzle and a man came in, muttering and pointing at the puzzle. I had no idea what he wanted, and couldn't even tell if he was upset or just trying to tell me something. His daughter arrived a few minutes later. We found out he used to be an engineer. As she translated his sounds and gestures, it turned out he was simply trying to give me tips on how to work a puzzle, edges first. Ugh. Heartbreaking! He used to be an engineer!"

We sighed together, laying there, and as more tears spilled, he continued to stay with my non-linear train of thought.

"Yeah," he said. "It's just painful to think about that kind of loss."

"Yes, it is. That's exactly it." I agreed. "And

that wasn't even the worst of it. I forgot to tell you this part. There was a different man I saw later that same trip, who apparently takes all his clothes off every night, strips the sheets off his bed, and begins running around. He came out, naked and confused, while I was trying to talk to the glazed-over orderly behind the counter. She had to rush off to deal with him!"

"Oh my God!" he exclaimed.

"I know. I just can't..." again I trailed off, not knowing how to finish my sentence.

Taking a breath, he tilted his head and asked, "Is this, all that you're saying, is this about dignity? Are you wanting dignity for those patients you met, and really needing to trust that your dad will have a sense of dignity as he declines?"

When he asked me that question, something lifted as one last stream of tears gave way. I felt a huge sense of relief flood my body, like when you finally lay down at the end of a long day.

"Yes... oh my gosh... Dignity..." I said, letting my mind sit with this thought. "That's it. I'm worried that he's not going to be held with dignity by us, or by the orderlies and doctors in the future. Yes. I want my dad's human dignity intact, no matter how he changes... Oh my God, that's totally it. Dignity!"

The conversation soon wrapped up but stayed with me, fresh, for the rest of the week. I was surprised to feel tangible reverberations of relief run through my body each time I reflected on it. A truth was somehow named. I can't explain why it mattered so much to be with this idea of dignity, this mantra, this promise to my dad. But it did. It mattered.

- Mary Goyer, www.consciouscommunication.co

Sitting on Opposite Sides of the Couch - Jim Manske

The main goal my partner, Jori, and I have as mediators is to cultivate equality and connection between two parties so that compassion is inspired in each of them. In the way we mediate, we don't put any overt attention on coming to specific resolutions.

We trust that once people are connected, compassionate giving & receiving will naturally occur, and that solutions will arise organically based on whatever needs are identified during the process.

So, on this particular day, we sat with a married couple who were really in a rough patch. They arrived at the mediation separately, at different times. One came into our mediation room and sat on one end of the couch where disputants typically sit. About five minutes later, the other partner arrived. She sat at the opposite end of the couch and they both settled in, leaning away from each other, pressing against their respective armrests. This gave us a lot of information, as we gauged their level of connection.

We explained our process and empathized right off the bat with what it might be like to come to a mediation, to be feeling so tender and unsure of what's going to happen in their relationship.

We began with our usual question. "Who is willing to listen first?" we asked.

There was a long silence; nobody really wanted to listen first.

This goes to a very important piece about empathy. Empathy has nothing to do with the words that we say and everything to do with where we put our attention. So, Jori and I stayed in that silent space, empathizing with our eyes, with our hearts, with how much these two people both desperately wanted to be understood and heard.

, he said, "I'm willing to listen first." So she proceeded to launch into her story of pain.

We all listened to and stayed with her as she spoke. We empathized out loud and reflected what we heard in terms of what her needs were. We got to this one essential need in that moment and said, "We'd like to carry this over to your husband and see if we can get him to reflect upon that. Is that okay with you?"

She said, "Yeah, that would be great."

So, we reported the need that we heard her mention, to make it easy for him. Let's just say the need was for understanding. He indicated that he'd be willing to reflect that same need as well, and he did.

We said, "Thank you." He'd just given us the gift of fulfilling our request so we expressed our heartfelt gratitude that he did that.

Then we asked him, "Now, what's coming up for you about this?" and he began telling his side of the story.

We listened to him for a while, acknowledged his experience, boiled things down to one essential point and did the same thing as before. We asked him for permission to carry this over to his partner. And she was able to reflect his primary need out loud. We just kept doing this little dance.

It's simple. But we call it a mediation dance where we collect a need from one person and carry it over like a gift on Christmas morning for the other person to unwrap... and we all find out how it is to receive that need, that gift.

For this couple, the dance went on for around forty-five minutes. If we'd taped it with a video camera, you'd have seen how their bodies stopped leaning away from each other as the process went on. Although their eyes stayed on us - they still refused to look at each other - their bodies began to relax.

Then, after an additional ten minutes of continued back-and-forth, we watched as they gradually started shifting in their seats so that their knees pointed towards each other. They still directed most of their comments to us, though, so we just kept the process moving forward.

The formula of finding the need, then reflecting it back, is almost like a mechanical process. It's really puzzling why it works, but it does! It connects people at the heart. And this couple was no exception.

They gradually, inch by inch, started moving towards each other. After another fifteen minutes of this process, this husband and wife actually started to talk directly to each other.

Jori and I backed off and let them talk to each other. Within another couple of minutes, they were holding hands and had their heads right next to each other, making an A shape. We couldn't hear a word of what they were saying but it didn't matter. They had connected.

They stayed in this cuddling position for at least another ten minutes, which felt almost timeless. It was just so delicious for me and Jori to be able to empathize with their hard-earned connection, after spending so much time empathizing with their pain. We had no idea what was being said, but it was really beautiful to be in the presence of that extended moment.

Finally, they kind of came back up. They made

eye contact with us and we just naturally went to the next part of the mediation process, asking them, "Who has an idea of what they'd like to do next?"

They decided that they needed to go have a meal together, a date. They hadn't had a date in weeks, no time to be with each other without the busy-ness of life. They walked out hand-in-hand and left one of the vehicles behind as they drove away.

That was the first step in a process that rebuilt their relationship. It took a few other mediations to get clear on some agreements and so forth, but they really built the quality of connection by being able to empathize with each other using our support.

This experience together gave them a renewed reference point for what had been lost when they first started blaming each other. They were able to get past that enemy image and remember the person they fell in love with. And for us to be able to support them through the process, and move past the pain they'd been stuck in, we savored that gift.

- Jim Manske, www.radicalcompassion.com

A Better Outcome - Sura Hart

I walked into my son's room where he was reading a book. My husband was out of town so I said, "Hey since Dad's away, I'd like to spend some extra time with you this weekend. Would you like to go to a movie with me tonight?"

He said, "No, I'm busy."

I had to breathe a moment. Just imagine if I had taken this "rejection" personally. He has time for other things. What's more important, a book or his mother? I didn't want to get into an argument.

Instead, I said, "Okay, so it looks like you're just really absorbed in that book."

"Yeah, it's getting really good."

"Okay, so tonight it sounds like you'd really rather just keep reading."

"Yeah, maybe I can finish it."

Not giving up on my need, I said, "I'm still interested in a movie or doing something else together on another night. How does that sound to you?"

"Fine. How about Sunday night? I know I'll be finished by then."

Ah, a win-win. These little exchanges might

seem kind of mundane, but they make a big difference in my relationship with my independent son.

- Sura Hart, adapted excerpt from Respectful Parents, Respectful Kids

Connecting With My Mom - LaShelle Lowe-Charde

The relationship with my mom had been strained since I entered adulthood. It consisted of a phone call once a month or so in which she told me what I should be doing and I told her what she should be doing. The conversations weren't very long and definitely not connecting for either of us.

After I had completed a year or so of intensive Non-Violent Communication (or NVC) training, I moved into a Zen monastery. With the support of this focused environment, it came to me that perhaps I could change the dynamic with my mom if I just offered empathy for everything she expressed. I knew this wouldn't be easy so I put some safety measures around it. I would only call when I was feeling clear-minded and resourced emotionally. I would get off the phone the moment I veered away from empathy. I would aim for a call once a week.

Before my first call, I reflected on the things my mom often said that I reacted to so I could try to prepare a new conversational pathway. The next time we spoke, it didn't take long before we went into some familiar themes.

"What do you want to live in a monastery for?" she asked. "You spent all that money on school and you're not making use of it."

I replied, "Yeah, confusing, huh? I'm guessing you want to know that I have security and everything I need. Is that right?"

"Well yeah. So why aren't you working?" she continued.

"Sounds like you're worried about me."

"Yes," she said. There was an awkward pause, then an immediate subject switch. "Are you going to check on your sister? She won't call me back."

I could have gone in for a direct answer, but I knew this was a layered subject. I asked, "It's scary when you don't know where she is and what she's doing, huh?"

"Yes, can you go check on her tomorrow?"

"Hmm, you really want some way to connect with her and know she is safe, is that it?"

And so we went. At some point I would start defending my decisions and as soon as I heard myself do that, I got off the phone. My mom didn't know what to do with the empathy at first. There were awkward pauses and her saying things like, "Why won't you answer me?!" with what seemed like a fair amount of frustration. I don't think she felt any more connected to me at first. For me, however, the results were immediate. I felt so much more alive and loving interacting with her in this way. I was relating in integrity and it was satisfying. But it was still difficult, of course.

Months went by with me calling her once a week or so and just offering empathy. Incrementally, I could hear a softening in her tone which I interpreted as her heart opening to me. Slowly she gave up on her "shoulds" for me, more and more easily.

Somewhere around the six-month mark, something new happened. She gave me the usual order to go check on my sister as she hadn't heard from her, and I responded with empathy as I had many times over the months, feeling her pain with her, letting it live in our interaction. Then, for the first time in my life, I heard my mom express a feeling, "Yeah, it really hurts," she said.

I froze as though a precious little bird had just alighted next to me. And then ever so gently I said, "Yeah, Mom I know it does, it hurts a lot."

Slowly, she began to express more feelings during our calls. Along with that emotional expression came genuine curiosity about my life and what was meaningful for me, something I had longed for over the years. I remember clearly the first moment she asked about my life in an authentic way even though it was fifteen years ago.

She asked, "Are you happy living at the monastery?"

"Yeah, Mom," I said.

"Okay, as long as you are happy," she acknowledged.

My mom and I enjoy a sweet and mutual love and respect these days. We talk on the phone frequently and I visit her several times a year. She has let me know that I am the only person in her life to whom she can tell anything.

-LaShelle Lowe-Charde, www.wiseheartpdx.org

A Father's Gift - Miki Kashtan

I was working with a woman, Sandra, whose dad was eighty-one years old and thinking about his upcoming death. He wanted Sandra to live in his house once he was gone. Which would've been great, except that she didn't want to. Although she liked the house, she couldn't live there because she was so full of fear when she was alone at night in the house, a fear she didn't understand, that she could not sleep there.

They had several conversations about this that went nowhere. He had been trying to convince Sandra, every time she was there, that it was a nice place, a paradise in his words, and that everybody was safe. Sandra was then repeatedly stuck with how to respond. She didn't want to lie to him and make promises she couldn't keep, and she was very clear that she wasn't going to live there. Whenever she did try to voice her concerns to him, he only redoubled his efforts to give her all the good reasons why it would be such a great idea: no rent, really nice place, and an amazing garden.

As I worked with her, I realized a big part of the issue was that she was doing the very same thing she said her father was doing, trying to explain herself and convince her dad that it simply wasn't possible. We worked for some time together to come up with an alternative way to imagine the conversation.

Here's what it could sound like:

"I want to come back to the topic that's been hard for us to talk about, about what happens to the house after you die. I've done a lot of thinking about it. And I want to start by telling you that I finally got it, how big the gift is that you're trying to give me. You want my happiness and you want me to live in what you think of as paradise, and I'm very touched. And I want to know if I got it; if this is really what is really motivating you.

So now I want to tell you what my big problem is. I wish I could receive your gift. Now that I really see how big it is and how beautiful it is, I wish I could receive it. The thing is, it's not a gift for me in this way, it's not paradise for me. I don't know why. I can't understand why I am always scared when I'm here. If I agree to what you want then it's possible that every night for the rest of my life I will not sleep well and I will be scared, all night long. I can't imagine this is what you want for me. (Pause) I want us to find some other way for this gift to come to me that works for me. Are you open to talking about it? Can you see why it can't work for me?"

As we developed this framing, Sandra was able

to relax in full and began to smile. The weight was finally being lifted off her. She was ready to go and speak with her dad with an open heart.

In parting, I would like to quote from Sandra's email to me after her conversation with her dad. It speaks for itself.

"I could see the relief in my Dad's face when he heard that I finally understood what a treasure he wants to give to me. At the end of the conversation he said it would be totally fine for him if we rent the house until any of us (me or my boys) would like to live there. I'm still touched! What I didn't expect at all is that, after we came to this place of really having heard each other, my resistance to living in the house decreased a little bit more with every passing day. I can almost imagine buying an Alarm System and a big dog and living there… hope it will not come so soon."

- *Miki Kashtan, www.thefearlessheart.org*

Kitty Empathy - Dian Killian

Several months ago, I passed by an ASPCA van, with cats up for adoption. I went over to take a look and fell in love with a cat called Caiden. I love Irish names, so he caught my attention. I already had two cats at home and wasn't looking for a third, but Caiden was so affectionate, such a lover boy sticking to me like Velcro, that I couldn't resist. He was like a baby just wanting to be held. So, Caiden came home with me.

My housemate was surprised and so were my two other cats. The ASPCA told me what to do when introducing them to each other and I followed all the steps diligently. I kept him in my room. I let him smell the other cats under the door. Everything seemed to be okay.

One day, though, Caiden clearly got tired of being kept to one room in the house. He escaped, got out into the main part of the house and all hell broke loose. I could never have guessed it, but this little guy, who was so warm, affectionate, and doting with me, was aggressive towards my other cats. When he got out of my room, he made a bee-line for my other male cat, and attacked immediately while Seamus screamed in terror. Horrified, I had to separate this giant ball of fur, an actual cat fight.

I shouted, "Stop it! Stop it! Leave him alone!" I felt so sad and concerned for Seamus. It was terrifying to watch how Caiden had hunted him down while the third cat hid in the closet.

For some time, the fighting continued between these two, though I tried to keep them separated. Even when I attempted to let them outside at different times, thinking this would give them some space, I would hear the howling and screaming of another fight from outside the house. I've grown up with cats, had them my whole life, and I've never seen anything like this.

It went on for weeks. I called the animal clinic, talked to their pet behavioral psychologist, discouraged. She said to me, "I hate to tell you this, but I think you better look for another home for Caiden. I don't think it's going to work out. The behavior you're describing, attacking the other cats, is kind of extreme. It doesn't bode well for working out long-term. Maybe Caiden needs to be a solo cat."

I sadly started looking for a new home for Caiden. I didn't really want to give him up so each time the two fought, I'd drop everything, and run over to stop it, hoping to make a difference. My housemate, I have to hand it to her, said, "Dian, I think you're actually making it worse because you get so scared when they fight."

It made sense. I hadn't thought about it before, but it's a natural phenomenon for fear to show up as aggression. I wondered if my fear was amping up the fight energy between the cats.

So, I completely changed my strategy. I began to pick Caiden up every time Seamus came inside the house. I pet him, loved him up, and said things like, "I just want you to know, I'm so glad you're here. I think over time you're going to like Seamus because he really enjoys being with other cats."

Seamus, upon entering and seeing the monster on my lap, was understandably tentative. Caiden would get a little antsy when the two were inside the same room, but I just kept up with the petting and the soothing voice, and tried to imagine how they both wanted some calmness and peace. After several days of this, they both relaxed. I still worried I might ultimately have to find another home for Caiden, but in time it was apparent that things truly had transformed.

Now, the two cats groom each other daily, sleep in the same bed (happily), play with each other, and even eat from the same bowl, which I never imagined would be possible. I wonder what the pet expert would think to see how things have changed. From my perspective, it really is an empathy miracle.

- Dian Killian, www.workcollaboratively.com

A Hit Instead of a Kiss - Mair Alight

I was visiting my son, who has two boys of his own, and trying to say goodbye at the end of the visit. As I leaned over to kiss my two-year-old grandson, he hit me in the face.

I was shocked and stood there, stunned. But immediately my son swooped up my grandson, held him, and said, "You're sad to see your Grandma go?"

My grandson started crying saying, "Yes, I don't want her to go!"

My son replied, "Yeah, you're sad and don't want her to go, but hitting her isn't the way to say that, honey."

He used a tender sweet voice as he patted my grandson's back. "I know you're sad. I know you don't want her to go but, in our family, we don't hit when we're upset. We use our words."

He was totally present with my grandson; no punitive mindset, just totally with him. With us both actually. Because next he reached out, put his hand on my shoulder, and said, "Mom, how about you? Are you okay?"

"Well yeah," I replied. "Just totally surprised. I wasn't expecting that, to get a hit instead of a kiss."

He was empathically with me and with his son in the same moment. How fortunate my grandsons are to have him for a father.

- Mair Alight, www.Mair@MairAlight.com

Empathy Cards During An Argument - Becka Kelley

When I met Daniel, he told me he had two emotions: angry and uncomfortable. It was only our first date, so I didn't push, but as an inner work junkie and very emotional person in general, I knew I would want to connect with him on a deeper emotional level.

At the beginning of our relationship, I was learning about Nonviolent Communication (NVC). As I practiced this style of communicating, sometimes he would feel angry saying, "Why can't you just talk like a normal person! All you're doing is answering me in questions!"

I, in return, would accuse, "You're problem solving and I want empathy!"

Around that time, I heard of an empathy card game called Grok and I thought it might offer a way of connecting that would work for both of us. In the game, there's one deck that lists a feeling on each card (like angry, sad, happy, etc.) and then another deck that lists a value for each card (like connection, safety, health, etc.). He was reluctant to try it at first, but eventually agreed to use the cards the next time we got into a disagreement.

The day came when Daniel told me he had agreed to watch the dog he once shared with an ex-girlfriend, while she was away. As he said this, I realized he'd made plans for the same weekend we had talked about going to a workshop together. When I reminded him about the workshop, and it seemed apparent that he had no intention of changing his plans with his ex, a lot of emotions, insecurities, and judgments arose for me. I also noticed Daniel sounded defensive as we talked about it, so we decided to use the Grok cards to help us work it out.

He went first, laying down three feelings cards: Torn, Overwhelmed, and Sad. He shared that Lily had called really concerned that she didn't have anyone to look after the dog. She wanted him to honor the commitment he'd made when they got the dog together. He felt sad that he had forgotten about the workshop and was worried this would cause a rift between us. He also missed his dog and wanted to spend time with her.

I then laid down some values cards, saying, "Are integrity and support really up for you right now? Wanting to honor your commitment to your dog and help out?"

He agreed and seemed more at ease. I continued, "Are you also wanting a connection between you and your dog because you miss her?"

He replied, "Yes, and it seems like you get

judgmental of me every time I spend time with her."

"So are you wanting a little more understanding about how important she is to you and the commitments you made?" I asked.

"Absolutely," he said and I saw his body relax.

When it was my turn, I laid down the cards: Disappointed, Worried, and Angry. I explained that I was really disappointed that we weren't going to the event together. I was really looking forward to it. I also recognized I was telling myself that he was choosing them over me, and that I felt angry and worried when I thought that way.

Daniel responded, "It's hard to hear that you're disappointed in me."

I said, "I'm not disappointed in you. I'm just disappointed. There's a difference." He said he hadn't ever thought there was a difference between the two.

When he laid out the values cards he chose: Security, Trust, and Intimacy.

He said, "It sounds like you were really looking forward to the closeness we would experience from going to this workshop together."

I nodded so he continued, "Are you wanting to feel secure in our relationship and trust that when I make plans with you that I will follow through?"

I noticed how I felt the pressure releasing in me as I heard his words. I answered, "Yes, definitely."

It was such a turning point in our relationship that we could have such a charged conflict and be able to practice seeing things from the other person's point of view. We felt so much closer after connecting in that way.

One day, I noticed he seemed to be upset about something. I asked him what was going on and he said, "I don't know! Just... get the cards!"

I attempted to hide my smile as I did so. I was so happy he was willing to be so brave and vulnerable in an effort to connect with me.

We no longer use the cards these days... we don't have to! He has developed an awareness of his emotions and is happy to empathize with me when I am in a struggle. I've grown in my ability to "talk like a normal person" when practicing empathy, and am better at focusing on listening instead of interrogating. We have developed a language we can use to connect to each other that is easy and deeply meaningful. We are so grateful!

- Becka Kelley, www.beckakelley.com

Blueberry Meltdown - Alan Seid

My home-office used to be in a little, teeny bedroom in the house, separated from my kids' play area with only a thin, hollow-core door.

One day, I was working in my office and I heard my daughter, who, at the time, was three. She was in the dining room and I heard some screaming, a tremendous tantrum-fit complete with yelling and kicking. So, I gave it a little time, but it just kept going and going. I knew my wife was with her, but things weren't shifting.

I was trying to focus and stay in the concentrated space I was in. The yelling, therefore, had me quite distracted and irritated.

So I charged out of my office thinking, "I need her to shut up!" That's what I was telling myself, "I need her to shut up. I need quiet."

I got within four feet of my daughter as I charged into the room. I didn't know what I was going to say, but it easily could have been something like, "What is wrong with you?!" or "Keep it down!" or something! But as I got close, something suddenly clicked. I think it had to do with years of practice in this. I just stopped, I took a deep breath, and I turned my attention inward.

In that pause, I repeated internally, I need her to

shut up.

Okay, that was at the surface. I need her to shut up.

If I got her to be quiet, then what would I have? What would that give me?

Well, really what's going on for me is that I'm needing a different level of support, and more quietness would really help that.

As soon as I got connected with my feelings and my needs, I felt something shift!

I was no longer on a war-path to get my child to shut up. I had gotten connected with myself and had felt a change.

Next, I found I was able to get present to her and get curious. I said, "Uh, what happened, what's going on?"

Well, it turned out that Mom had given her a bowl of blueberries with milk, and several blueberries had fallen out of the bowl and onto the floor. In her three-year-old mind, this had shattered the perfection of this bowl of blueberries.

I asked her, "If I get you three more blueberries out of the freezer, will that help?"

"Yeah!" she said.

So I got her three more blueberries, and her

crying stopped, the tantrum stopped, and all the kicking stopped as well.

It wasn't about me going for my outcome of quiet that did the trick, I don't think. It was about me going for connection. And then sitting with the question: what can we do here that would meet both of our needs?

Self-empathy helps me have that kind of shift. In the long run, if I didn't have those skills, I might have a very different connection with my children, because they might see me as this irritable ogre, rather than someone who is willing to self-connect, slow down, and think, "What's going on? Okay, if there's a strategy here, let's find it."

That's the difference. That's the kind of easy shift I can have with self-empathy. And those little shifts make a big impact in my relationships.

- Alan Seid, www.cascadiaworkshops.com

Overwhelmed Granny - Anne Walton

My youngest granddaughters spent a lot of time hanging out with me when they were young. There were enjoyable moments and challenging ones, too. The following took place when they were about eight and ten years old.

Typically, they played together fairly well but then every so often, things would devolve.

It would begin with Samantha, the younger one, calling out, "Granny, Jessica's being mean to me!"

These few simple words seemed, inevitably, to inspire Jessica to take it up a notch or two.

As soon as I heard this plaintive tone of Sam's, I'd feel overwhelmed and discouraged. "Oh no, here we go again!" I'd think. The timing of this interchange would always occur when I was tired and not very resourceful. I'd start praying for their parents to arrive to take them home, like the day was essentially over.

Once they'd gone home, I'd feel relief at getting them out of my hair, but then the self-blaming and criticism would begin. *I'm a terrible Grandmother. Grandparents aren't supposed to get like this; it's supposed to be all dreamy and wonderful. They're my grandchildren! I'm supposed to love them unconditionally and never feel irritated or impatient! Nothing like this happens for any other Grandmothers - only me.*

Then one day, after I'd attended a communication workshop, something different happened. As the girls began to bicker, it occurred to me to try listening to them as I'd heard about in the workshop. I took a breath, noticed that familiar hopelessness, and definitely noticed that I wanted to shout, "Oh for heaven's sake, stop it. Why don't you get along?"

But, in that moment, I didn't. Instead, I took some deep breaths and said something like, "Gosh, are you feeling kind of sad, Samantha?"

Suddenly, it was a different world in my house. I was able to take another breath and do some kind of reflection with her. "What was it that happened?"

We did a little investigation together about why they were on each other's cases. And I felt resourceful, at least a little bit. It was just enough to get me through the moment. I was amazed to see that I had a different option than the usual, Oh good grief, they're fighting again. I wish their parents would hurry up and get here.

I'm glad I can laugh about it now. It took time to realize that it was okay to feel irritated and to wish they'd stop fighting. I was just a human being doing the best I knew with a couple of kids. It was also nice to learn I could do things in a different way than in the past, which helped me connect with my granddaughters more easily on those harder days.

- Anne Walton, www.chooseconnection.com

Hating School - Cedar Rose Selenite

Last year, our family took on a "homeschooled-girl-tries-out-school-and-hates-it" experiment. My eleven-year-old daughter had wanted to go to school, but after a few weeks she'd changed her mind. I drove her to the drop-off point one morning and she refused to go into class.

Her dad and I were quite eager for her to stick with the idea for a while, though. Her being at school allowed me to work more hours and have more sustainability. So when she looked like she was going to change her mind, on the morning drive no less, it threw me off.

We sat down outside the building and I asked her, "Sweetie, what's going on?"

"I don't feel like it," she replied. She said she *might* be getting sick.

I told her that people who go to school often don't feel like it. And, I went on, they even go when they are tired or have a slight cold.

"Honey," I said. "Daddy really wants you to go! I want you to! What is it that you don't enjoy about it? Is it your teacher? The kids?"

She exploded at me. *"Mom! I just want empathy!"*

I sat in silence, stunned. Time stopped for me. The universe waited. I began to cry.

You see, around the time my baby girl turned four years old, I began studying the key principles of connection. I put a lot of attention - for years - on the way I wanted to be with others in my life, and how I wanted to show up for my family.

I focused hours of energy learning about being with people in full presence: listening to their experience, intuitively guessing their deepest needs, and sharing my most authentic truth. These were all values I'd hoped to pass on to my children: the importance of compassion, the power of empathy… the impact of giving and receiving it.

So when I cried, I wasn't crying because I had failed to offer her empathy. I had compassion for myself for that. And I wasn't crying because she was angry with me.

I had tears in my eyes in that moment because of a realization. I was overwhelmed by the most profound sense that I'd attained the thing I'd most wanted to accomplish as a parent. I had, in fact, taught my child to expect empathy. And to ask for it when it wasn't happening. To me, this was huge.

I wiped my tears away, took a breath, and shifted gears.

At that point, I didn't care about anything else in the world. I said, "You're so sad and just want me to listen?"

She nodded her head. I proceeded to ask her if she was feeling tired. I really wanted to understand. I asked if she just wanted to rest and have a choice about school. She nodded again.

She did decide, after a few minutes, to go to class that day. And she did so with willingness. I suppose she just needed a moment to be heard, first. Those moments outside the school gave me hope for the world. If every child could experience empathy and collaboration, and not simply be told what to do every time an adult is in a rush, the world could be a very different place.

- Cedar Rose Selenite, universalhumanneeds.org

Unsolicited Advice - Mark Schneider

I was going through an extremely challenging and painful divorce process. My sense of fairness, financial security, and even sharing a common "world view" with my soon-to-be ex-wife was being challenged in the biggest possible ways. One incredibly stressful issue was our living situation. My ex was still occupying the house that I owned, purchased prior to us getting married, and she wouldn't leave or offer any money for rent. I wanted to get renters into the place in order to afford the monthly mortgage.

One day, via text, my best friend offered his suggestion about the whole situation. "Why don't you just move back into the house, since it's yours, even if she's still living there? That will make her uncomfortable and she'll get out."

I ignored it at first, but when we spoke on the phone, shortly thereafter, the unsolicited advice amped up.

He said, "Let's move you into your house today, with her still in the house. Seriously. I think that being willing to face present moment pain, and not avoid what needs to be done, is good relationship and life wisdom."

"No, I'm not going to move in today, but I'm

glad you reminded me of that possibility. I'll take a look at that option and see if there are any legal implications."

"Listen," he replied. "She's not uncomfortable enough! She will leave if you make her very uncomfortable. It's moving right into the fire to be in your house. Conflict yes, but better that way than through lawyers. It's like dealing with things on a direct level! Maybe go make love with a woman in your house, where your ex will have to listen to it... Please don't rule these ideas out. You'll save lots of money by using your wits."

"Look," I said, "I'm not averse to considering the possibility of moving in. I also want to make sure that I'm not going to hurt my case, or get a restraining order against me. I need to figure out what's involved. There are some psychological challenges for me in that scenario, too. I don't know if I have it in me to face that much conflict and dissonance."

"Well, I think it's a great fucking idea. It's the perfect idea. Hard to imagine a restraining order could apply. You aren't harassing her. You're just moving back in."

"I discussed this scenario with someone, and I recall mention of 'automatic' restraining orders being in place under certain circumstances when couples separate. I need to check it out."

"She needs to be uncomfortable. How about a hot tub at 2am? Find out. But do it anyways. She needs this. And it will be good for you!"

"Ok. Enough." I said. "I'd request no more advice on this. I understand your position."

"If you don't do something, my respect for you will waver," he countered.

"Super unsupportive."

"Not true! The truth is, you created this. Only you can go into that lair and slay that dragon, unarmed with lawyers. You're being chicken shit."

I was incredulous, but so was he, it seemed.

"I'm done," he said. "I'm going to work to help folks deal with seriously fucking real problems now. Without lawyers! Done! Goodbye."

I sighed, took a breath, and said, "I'm working so damn hard on this divorce thing. I'm doing everything I know how, using my best intelligence. Hearing from my dear friend that his respect for me is going to waiver if I don't take action along the lines that he sees fit is not what I need right now. And then you follow-up calling me 'chicken shit'?! I feel very hurt, sad, and angry by that."

He responded, "Hey, listen. Whatever you

choose to do."

And with that, the conversation was over. I spent the next hour using all the self-connection tools I could think of to help me navigate the intense feelings and thoughts I was having. I decided to reach out and see what I could do about this little interaction from my side of things.

"Hey," I said when I called him back a bit later. "I did a little work around our conflict, and I'm imagining that it is very frustrating for you, and all those who know me, to witness the kind of bullshit that my ex is putting me through and getting away with. I imagine that's what motivated some of your strong opinions and statements."

I felt a calmness come back in between us immediately as he said, "Very insightful. That's exactly it. By the way, beautiful communication skills."

"Thanks. To be honest, I'm kind of impressed myself with this one. It would have been easy to stay in reaction, but using what I've been learning about empathy, I thought to consider what needs of yours might be under all this, and that helped me interpret what you were saying as coming from a desire, at the core, for fairness, for justice, and a true concern for me."

"Yes, exactly! I'm feeling a heightened sense

of injustice for you. You are my closest friend and it seems so mean what she is trying to pull off. I apologize for taking it too far. I'm sorry. I'm here to support you in whatever way I can."

And from there, we were able to get back on track and get on with our day.

A Time Out For Reflection - Mair Alight

My six-year-old grandson, Anton, went with me to the science museum and was just beside himself with excitement. When we arrived, he played on the red ropes at the entrance. Then he took off, running into the crowd, dodging people and disappearing. When I saw him again, he was swinging on the red ropes while people were trying to move through the line, and I said very sharply, "Anton, get over here right now!"

He had been having so much fun on the rope, but when I yelled, he instantly crumpled at the sound of my voice. He came over to me with his head down so low.

I said, "I need a time-out here."

"Okay," he replied, and he looked around to see where he might sit.

I smiled wryly and exclaimed, "Not for you, for me!"

He looked at me with big eyes and said, "What?!"

"I don't like the way I just talked to you." I replied. "I wouldn't want to talk to anyone that way, especially not my beloved grandson. So I'm giving myself a time out right now to think it over."

He was truly stupefied, looking at me in wonder while I sat myself down on the floor right there in the line, against the wall. He sat as near to me as he possibly could, curled up to me, leaning right on my leg. I sat there for several minutes, quietly.

Then I said, "Well, that was about five minutes. I think I learned my lesson because I've been thinking it over."

He just continued to look at me with bewilderment in his eyes and I said, "Do you think I learned my lesson?"

He shook his head very solemnly and said, "Yes."

So I suggested, "Well then, why don't we go have a fun time at the science center?" We both jumped up and went on our way.

I imagine people would think I was in the right to scold him when he was running around. But to me, he was just a kid being a kid. I still wanted to explain to him a little more about my perspective, so a little later that morning I did.

"Look," I said, "I want to tell you why I was upset earlier."

He seemed totally willing to hear it.

"It was because I was scared when I didn't

know where you were. Then when I saw you on the ropes, pulling, I was worried they were going to fall over, and hurt yourself or someone else."

He totally got it. He nodded, and I truly had the sense that we connected completely differently than we would have if I'd tried to convey the same thing earlier in a sharp, intense way.

- *Mair Alight, www.Mair@MairAlight.com*

Teenage Gratitude - Penny Wassman

My partner had photographed my teenage daughter receiving the winner's trophy at a sporting event. Thinking she would be delighted, he enlarged, framed, and then placed the photo on a table in our entrance hallway.

I was relieved he wasn't home when my daughter first saw it. She took one look at the photo and exclaimed, "Who took that photo?! It's crap!"

I couldn't believe it! *How ungrateful! How selfish can she be?! Doesn't she realize the love that went into creating this gift?!* All kinds of things flashed through my mind at that moment. I even wondered what kind of mother I was to bring up such a "selfish" child.

Luckily, I'd attended an introductory communication workshop the night before and the facilitator had talked about the idea that *all violence is a tragic expression of unmet needs.* I was certainly experiencing her words as rude… but what needs were underlying them? I remembered hearing that one important need for teenagers, in particular, is "choice."

I also remembered that, no matter what was being said, her outburst was not about me. So I followed the instruction that had been given at the workshop for these kinds of moments and I took a deep breath. I actually took two. I used that time to get in touch with my own need for recognition of my husband's love in putting the picture together.

And then, feeling somewhat tentative, I asked my daughter, "So you would really like to choose the pictures that are displayed of you?"

"Yes!" she exclaimed. "Dad should have asked me first. It's a stupid picture!"

Taking another breath, I decided to stay with the same theme. "Choice" was the only thing I could think of.

"So I guess you're really frustrated and having choice is important to you?" I asked.

Apparently, I was somewhat on track. I heard her mumble, "Uh-huh."

She looked down at the table, silently, her shoulders sagging. Still feeling confused and unsure of the next best step, I asked her if it would be okay if I put the photo in her Dad's office. She agreed.

When I returned to the table where we had been having the discussion, I discovered my daughter with her head in her arms, sobbing. Between sobs, she looked up at me and said, "It's not about the picture… it's about…"

And she began to tell me about a work

experience she had endured that day that had been very painful for her. I listened quietly, feeling immense gratitude for the few prompts I'd learned that made space for this moment.

I can imagine what might have happened if I'd expressed my earlier thoughts about her being ungrateful and selfish when she was already feeling so raw and tender.

Instead, because I had been willing to look for something behind the words I had initially found so challenging, I had a treasured opportunity to be of support and to deepen the connection between us. That, I think, is precious. Especially with a teenager!

After my daughter had recovered, she asked me, "Where did you put the picture?"

I told her it was in her Dad's office.

"Oh," she replied. "Let's put it back in the hallway... it's really okay."

The photo has been proudly displayed there, front and center, ever since.

- Penny Wassman, www.pennywassman.ca

Different Ways of Showing Love - Kristin Masters

When my wife and I bought our house, I was pregnant, so we were under a time constraint to get things done before the baby came. We agreed on some of the priorities, knowing we wouldn't have time to complete everything until after the baby was born. But certain things were important. We knew, for instance, that we'd need to have a bathroom before we had a home birth. The problem was, my wife was a bit of a perfectionist.

She paid attention to detail like no one else I'd ever met. She had quite the woodworking skills, so she took charge of most of the projects. She would work on getting the cabinets in, send me off to do something, and I was to come back right away to assist with the next step. This setup worked most of the time, but as we both felt the pressure of the ticking clock, we got annoyed with each other.

"Would you go measure this?" she asked. "It's going to go right here, so measure it."

A few minutes later, my reply, "It's about twelve and a half inches."

"No, I need to know what it is to the sixty-fourth of an inch. That's what measuring is."

"Ok. It's twelve and a half."

And so it went. She would get irritated at me for my sloppy measuring, which made some sense because, in fact, I was a sloppy measurer. I didn't even know sixty-fourths were marked on a tape measure. I'd never counted them before.

Re-measuring the cabinets, she got so frustrated. "You know, I have to do this right. You've gotta be more precise when you're helping with these things."

"It's underneath, nobody is going to see it anyway!" I replied.

That sent her into a fit of fire-spitting and the like. At some point, after we decided I should stay away from the tasks involving measuring, I figured out something relevant to the big picture. I began to get what her precision was really about.

"Is it that you just really want this bathroom to be beautiful and functional, and all of the pieces to fit together nicely?"

"Yes, yes!" she said. "You need to measure to the sixty-fourth of an inch!"

Suddenly the story in my head that she was too picky, too anal compulsive, etc., gave way even more. This was her way of making sure she was doing everything well so it'd last. It was a gift to me and our baby.

"Yeah, you want this to be beautiful. You want us to live in this house for a very long time, and you want all of the pieces to fit together."

She breathed and all of the sudden it felt like there was an exhale in the space itself. The air in the room, that was electrically charged and mean just minutes before, softened immediately. We smiled at each other and at our wonderful new home.

- Kristin Masters, www.nvcsantacruz.org

Whining Kids - Sura Hart

A huge issue around my house has always been whining. At the time I experienced a shift in my perception, my children were ages four, seven, and ten.

It seemed to me, before then, that they whined all the time. It drove me crazy. Whenever I heard that whiny sound in their voices, I immediately wanted to stop whatever I was doing so I could make *it* stop.

Then, I went to a parenting workshop away from my home where I learned that all people are ever doing is expressing their needs. After I returned, I noticed that the first time my daughter whined to me was when she was requesting something from me. I suddenly realized that she whined whenever she was expecting me to reject or deny her request.

I also realized that she was used to having to ask for things, and that she was accustomed to me saying no to her requests. It became obvious to me that, in our interactions, my daughter was often powerless to get something that she wanted.

I immediately felt a huge wave of compassion for her. I also saw how my parenting had not expressed respect for the autonomy needs of any of my children.

What I earlier thought of as whining was their way of trying to be fully heard and to rebel against what I suddenly saw as my lack of respect for their autonomy.

When I fully realized all of this, I felt regret and sadness that my relations with my children had so little trust and respect.

I sat down and talked with my kids openly about my thoughts and realizations. I let them know that I very much wanted to listen to them better and to work on growing more trust between us. When I finished, my kids looked at me as though I had come from an alien planet. My four-year-old began to cry.

However, within just three weeks after my talk with them, the whining behavior has dramatically decreased, and my children and I have very much enjoyed each other's company.

- Sura Hart - adapted excerpt from <u>Respectful Parents, Respectful Kids</u>

Bike-Riding Mishap - Jean Morrison

On a visit with my daughter, while she was in college, we decided to try out an old funky bicycle-built-for-two that a friend had given her. We weren't even that sure of its ride-ability, but thought it might be fun.

She was having a kind of grumpy day (early morning, not enough sleep, etc.) but we got on the bike—her in front, me in back—and off we rode.

Within a few minutes, we were moving along quickly. Soon, there was a situation where my instincts simultaneously prompted me to yell, "Brake!" and to backpedal in an attempt to slow the bike down.

It didn't work.

Instead of braking, the chain jumped off the sprockets and we immediately came to a scary stop, falling in a grassy area.

We were safe but my daughter was livid. "What were you thinking?!" she fumed, and continued shouting angrily.

Even though this was some time ago, I remember a calmness coming over me, a feeling of "dropping into my body." I knew her anger resulted from the shock and fear of the unexpected and lurching stop. But she really was quite upset, and seemed to think it was all my fault. The ride looked like it might be ruined as she started to stomp away.

I stayed with the calmness in my body of silent empathy for her, then called out something like, "You're upset and not sure you feel like riding more?"

She nodded, almost imperceptibly, and I continued, "Yeah, that was surprising and pretty scary!"

I waited another moment, then owned my part of "messing up" by acknowledging that what I did had, in fact, landed us in the grass. And then I invited her to help me get the chain back on so we could continue to ride.

She immediately walked over to me and the bike, crouched down, and we worked together to put the chain back on. Within a few minutes, we were ready to continue the ride. What could've been a disastrous interaction, turned into one of repair and re-connection.

- Jean Morrison, www.nvcsantacruz.org

The Little Lamb - Aya Caspi

It was a Saturday evening when I heard the kids' excited voices as they were approaching the house and calling me, "A-ya... A-ya…"

"What? What?" I asked as I rushed to the door.

When I opened it, I saw Michael, my son, standing on the stairs with a little lamb in his arms.

"What is this?!" I exclaimed.

"It's a little lamb." he said with sadness in his voice. "She was born yesterday and her mother doesn't let her near. She is very weak. She may die."

Michael came in with the tiny lamb, followed by Dan-Dan, his brother, and Deon, a friend.

Before I had a chance to say anything, they laid her down on their spider-man blanket and covered her with an old rug.

The baby lamb didn't look so good. She couldn't stand on her feet and her eyes were gazing at one imaginary point.

"We took her to Rebeca." said Shahar, my husband, as he came through the door. "She said that these things happen from time to time. We found her too late and there isn't much chance that she will survive because she needs her mother's milk to strengthen her immune system. But we can try to give her some cow milk from a bottle."

And then he added, "I need to go soon. Will you take care of it?"

To my own (untrained) ears, it didn't sound like I had any choice... but this is another topic for another time. As I sat for a bit with the four kids and, apparently, a dying lamb in the house, I noticed how much I wanted her to live. My heart was full with compassion for the fragile creature which had just landed in my life. I realized I was willing to do whatever I could to help her survive. And I was not the only one.

Forty-year-old me, eight-year-old Michael, six-year-old Deon, five-year-old Dan-Dan, and little three-year-old Dana all had the same response: unconditional love and care for the helpless, vulnerable animal baby.

As Dan-Dan put it, "Aya, I can't stop thinking about the lamb, and I don't know why."

"I can understand that Dan-Dan," I said, "because I'm feeling the same as you. I am having frequent thoughts about her, too. I believe it is in our human nature to feel compassion when we are facing life in its vulnerability. We humans care. This is how we are."

Michael seemed to appoint himself as "in

charge" and he began feeding her with a bottle. But the lamb was too weak to suck from it.

"She will live, right Aya?" he implored. "She has to live!" he said, desperately looking at me for reassurance.

"We just need to feed her and love her and she will live" he continued, as if this was a matter of negotiation.

"Me and Dana even told her that we love her. And I made a wish with a wish flower."

"I don't know, Michael" I responded. "Sometimes these things happen. Sometimes newborn babies do not survive..." I trailed off, uncomfortable with the words that were struggling to come out of my mouth.

In that moment, I suddenly realized that I was feeling really helpless and afraid, and was trying to "rescue" Michael and myself from the potential pain of the loss of the lamb. I was also hoping to avoid the pain of witnessing my beloved son's heartbreak out of helplessness in the face of death.

I could see how wanting to protect us both led me to trying to take him away from his full experience by telling him, "This is how things are. Babies sometimes die."

In effect I was sending him the message that he

should not feel afraid or helpless, because they are weaknesses, and that he should protect himself with reason. Part of me wanted him avoiding his feelings so that his heart would not be broken-open.

But then I was hit with the full awareness of the price! Disconnecting from his own humanity, from his vulnerability. Shutting down his heart - where life itself resides - in order to protect from pain?

No.

I *don't* want to protect him from his heart break. I want him, and everybody else for that matter, to experience the aliveness, strength, and empowerment that are gained both from being present with our hearts under all circumstances and from opening ourselves fully to any experience in the moment. How else can anyone truly live the life they were meant to live?

As I quickly became conscious of all of this, I knew I wanted to change directions. I wanted to offer Michael the experience of being met where he was, of being understood and accepted for what he was feeling and needing in that moment in time.

How I long to offer this gift to my children on a regular basis!

And so this is what I said to him.

"Michael," I said, "My heart is touched deeply

by how much you care about this little creature. I see how you want to protect her life. You are willing to do whatever is needed to save her, and I can imagine how helpless and distressed you feel when you neither have the certainty nor the power to decide what will be the end results of your efforts.

Michael's tears confirmed my understanding. He hugged me and cried quietly. I felt relieved and grateful for making this turn on time, as I could support him in connecting with his feelings, by offering my understanding of what it was like for him, instead of trying to distract him from his helplessness and fear, contributing to him adding a layer of protection to his heart. I remembered Marshall Rosenberg's words about learning to enjoy somebody else's pain. Finally, I got what he meant. It was the sweet pain of being with what was real, with being with What Is. For the first time ever, I was enjoying my son's tears.

As I sensed that Michael was complete with being understood, I decided to offer him a piece of education.

"You know, Michael, I feel peaceful when I am doing everything that is within my power to show up for what matters to me, which is, in this case, to care for life in all its forms and protect it as best I can.

And as far as I can tell, you are doing the same. We have taken the lamb into our house, offered her food and shelter, love and care. I think this is all we can do. Whether she is to live or not, is not in our hands. And therefore I'm letting go of being "in charge" of it.

When I'm able to let go of worrying whether my efforts will bring my desired results or not, I notice that I can focus my energy fully on responding to the situation with all the power I have to invite what I long for. Letting go of having to have what I want to happen, frees me to do whatever my heart is really moved to do in the situation, and therefore I have no regrets later on.

Does this make any sense to you?"

"Yes Aya, I'm doing everything I can. There is really nothing else to be done. And if she dies I will bury her myself and I will look for the most beautiful stone to be put on top of her grave so I will know where it is. Look at her Aya, isn't she beautiful?"

I nodded my head as we continued feeding the little lamb and petting her.

She survived the night but died the next day.

Michael and Dan-Dan buried her in the

backyard and put the wood sword that Dan-Dan made in preschool on top of it. It made a perfect cross.

On top of the sword Michael put his pink crystal stone. I watched both of them from the porch as they leaned forward to the ground and silently sent the little lamb to her next journey with an open heart.

I stayed there for a few more minutes, taking it all in, grateful for the rich connection, learning, and meaning we all took from the little lamb's short appearance in our lives.

- Aya Caspi, www.cnvc.org/user/ayacaspi44

Inner-Child Rescue - Sarah Peyton

I was working in a class with a young woman who was having a difficult time with certain aspects of parenting her young child. When her daughter felt angry, it was scary for this woman. She couldn't stay in relationship or even function very well in those moments. She'd just freeze.

I found out she, herself, had grown up in a situation where her relationship with her mom had been quite dangerous and not at all supportive of well-being. This woman's own mother had, in fact, severely beaten her during bursts of anger; beaten her so badly that the police were called.

We went on to do something I call "time travel empathy," in which there's an internal dialogue, or an inner-part "rescue" of sorts. It goes by different names, but it's a way of working with the parts of our brains that have remained alive to old experiences. When past incidents have not been resolved, they stay awake in the memory, which is sort of the basic foundational starting point of post-traumatic stress, and they remain alive in our bodies, as well.

I asked this woman if she would be willing to go back in time and do a rescue for the little one in her who had been in such danger, and that's what we did. We traveled back in time. We froze time to make the environment safe and we froze her mother so that her mother was immobilized. We laid her mother down and put a sheet over her so that there was no longer any visual cue of her mother's anger and scariness in the room. Then we sat with this inner-little girl and made empathy guesses for her.

We guessed that she was really scared, first and foremost. And we wondered if she was needing to know that she was being seen, that she existed, and that her needs mattered. We touched on her frozenness, terror, overwhelm, physical pain, and helplessness.

As we did this, the woman recognized how much her inner-child needed, even in hindsight, to be protected, to have acknowledgment that no one expects their mother to be a source of pain or terror.

I just kept asking her to tune into this image of her own body as a little girl, and as we made these guesses, the little girl uncurled from a fetal position and slowly stood up. The woman who was receiving empathy "watched" the unfolding and said, "Oh my goodness, she's so strong!"

I asked if she wanted to bring this previous self up to the present time. Of course, the actual fact is she'd already survived all of these years of her life. She did not need to live them again. This little one, trapped in a memory, was simply that: trapped. She was caught in that past moment because it was so hard and she was unaccompanied there. So, we invited this little one to come back to present time. She was very willing to do so, and slipped through time and space back to the here-and-now. The woman was so relieved to have her own little one back with her.

Next, I said, "Now, when you think about your own daughter's face when she's angry, what is it like? How is it to feel into your daughter being angry?"

She said, "Oh, she's just a little girl. She looks like me and she looks like her dad. She doesn't just look like her Grandma. I wonder what she's so angry about."

It seemed clear, after having time travelled, that this woman had a very different sense of her own child's anger. I was able to connect with her about a month later because I was curious to see if her new experience was a stable one.

She said, "Yes! I'm really not frightened of my daughter when she gets upset anymore!"

I think this speaks on so many levels to the power of empathy to change lives and support people's well-being.

- Sarah Peyton, www.empathybrain.com

Empathy at Work: Creating a Culture of Compassion

Misbehaving for the Substitute - Victoria Kindle Hodson

The librarian of Lincoln Elementary School sent a note to Ms. Jackson, a 3rd-grade teacher, who'd recently been out sick, telling how "noisy, rude, and disrespectful" her class was during their library visit with the substitute teacher.

When Ms. Jackson returned to school, she was curious to find out what had happened with her usually considerate students. I was there to help facilitate this discussion using some of the tools we'd been introducing to the students, from *The No-Fault Classroom* curriculum.

Ms. Jackson started by having students get their "empathy mats" and feelings & needs card decks from their cubbies. They hustled their way to the back of the room and grabbed their manila envelopes.

Ms. Jackson sat on a low chair with her students arranged around her on the floor in a large circle, read the librarian's note aloud, and asked, "What does Mrs. Ladd mean when she says you were noisy, rude, and disrespectful? What were you doing?"

The students, visibly concerned, blurted out their responses including: We talked a lot. Our voices were louder than they're supposed to be in the library. We didn't stop talking when the substitute teacher told us to. Some people drew on the bookshelves. We didn't put away our books, and somebody ripped up paper and left the pieces on the floor.

"Okay." Ms. Jackson continued, "Thinking back on what happened in the library, how do you feel about it now? Please go through your feelings card decks and choose cards that describe the feelings that are coming up for you."

Papers rustled purposefully and students murmured quietly. They had sorted their feelings in this way many times during the year, and they were confidently selecting and placing cards on their mats.

Ms. Jackson went on when they looked ready, "So, what needs of yours were or were not met by what everyone in the class did in the library? Please place your needs cards on your mat." Their small hands deftly ruffled through the needs card decks, stopping now and then to draw a card and place it on a mat.

"Who," she asked, "would like to share

feelings and needs about what happened in the library?"

Molly looked at the cards in front of her, then spoke up to say she felt sad and embarrassed because respect and cooperation are needs that are important to her, and she realized that she hadn't been respectful or cooperative with the substitute teacher or Mrs. Ladd. Juan agreed and said he was shocked that the class had acted the way it did. Olivia jumped up to say she felt angry because she wanted to be heard and that she had tried to get people to stop, but no one would listen to her. Kim wasn't sure she wanted to say anything but then finally did.

"I want things to be fair," she said sadly. "We weren't fair to Mrs. Ladd or the substitute."

The students had a lot to say, and this kind of sharing went on for several minutes. The talk was very general. No one was taking responsibility for what happened... or making accusations.

I leaned over to Ms. Jackson to make a suggestion. She turned back to the students and asked, "When some kids were drawing on shelves, talking loudly, and dropping scraps of paper on the floor, what do you think their feelings and needs were? Can you think about what was up for the people doing these things?"

Suddenly, emotional floodgates opened, and before anyone had a chance to put cards on their mats, the students who had done these things began identifying themselves and excitedly sharing their feelings and needs. Jed said there were three classes in the library at once, and it was too hot and crowded for him. He said he was frustrated and upset that it was so uncomfortable, and he was going to have to be there a long time. Heather admitted to ripping up a paper she had been given and throwing the pieces at the wastebasket. She saw that some pieces missed, but at the time she didn't care. She said she was impatient because she didn't even know why the class was in the library and what they were supposed to be doing. Aaron explained that he started doodling on the bookshelves because he felt discouraged and hopeless when he couldn't find the books he wanted, and there wasn't anyone to help him. It was in pencil, and he meant to erase it but didn't have time.

After several more minutes of this kind of spontaneous, specific, heartfelt sharing, Ms. Jackson continued, "I hear that some of you felt confused, uncomfortable, anxious, and frustrated. Is there more?"

"Shut down," shouted Chang. "There was no one to talk to about what was going on in me, so I just stopped listening."

"All right," Ms. Jackson replied, "so, shut down is another feeling that came up. I'm hearing that all of these feelings came up because you wanted to be heard and to be clear about what to do, because you had questions and needed help and support, because you wanted understanding about what was going on in you, and because you needed to be more comfortable in the library that was way too crowded and hot. Is there anything more?"

No one spoke.

"Now that you understand your feelings and needs," Ms. Jackson continued, "can you think of something you wish you had done instead of what you did?"

Another wave of responses: I wish I had picked up a book, sat in a corner and read. I wish I had just worked on my homework. I wish I had asked if I could work in the hallway. I wish I had asked Jason to help me find the book I wanted. I wish I had drawn pictures on my own notebook paper instead of on the shelves. I wish I had walked over to the wastebasket and put the papers in.

Ms. Jackson nodded and said, "Please, keep these ideas in mind next time you feel stressed and unable to tell anyone about your frustration. Now, with Mrs. Ladd's note in mind, what shall we do next?"

Yet another floodgate opened, and everyone had something they wanted to do for Mrs. Ladd: Let's ask her what we can do to make it up to her. Let's write her a note. Let's make a pretty card to put it in. Let's have everyone sign it. Let's have her come to our room and someone can read the note to her here. Let's clean the bookshelves in the library. Let's have an appreciation party for her. Let's do all of those things! Let's write a note to the substitute teacher, too.

Excitement filled the air as students brainstormed about how to reconnect with both the librarian and the substitute teacher. Ms. Jackson divided them into groups to take on these tasks, and they spent much of the afternoon happily carrying out their plans.

- Victoria Kindle Hodson, www.thenofaultzone.com

One Versus the Committee - Kevin Goyer

I was asked to sit on a hiring panel for our special education department. We were looking for several new positions, including an Instructional Assistant who would work in a specific special education classroom all day alongside the main teacher.

After we interviewed three candidates for the Instructional Assistant position, we had an opportunity to discuss our impressions with Roy, the teacher this person would be working with, who also sat on the panel.

When we asked him what he thought, I was surprised to learn that Roy was leaning toward a particular person, applicant three, who had not stood out to me at all. In fact, she'd performed so poorly during her interview, one of the other panelists thought she'd deliberately sabotaged it. Her answers to the interview questions were short and vague; I didn't think they inspired much confidence in her.

Every person on the panel, other than Roy, went around the table sharing reasons why they felt applicant three was not qualified to work with Special Ed students based on her interview responses. But as we went on to talk about the other two applicants, and the qualities they displayed during their interviews, he kept going back to how strongly he felt we should hire applicant three.

Now, we were all well aware that he had a higher stake in the decision because the new hire would be working directly with him all day. And I happened to know that he had a good impression of this applicant because he'd worked with her before and he knew some of the strong qualities that she exhibited as a substitute I.A. in his room. We all got that. It was just difficult for any of us to follow his reasoning based on the evaluation tool we were required to use during hiring.

As we weighed, for example, the importance of paperwork and organizational skills against the interpersonal skills needed to work with a student population, he seemed to contradict himself. First, he said one thing about how "trainable" some of these skills were, in reference to his top choice applicant. Later, he said the opposite, that these things couldn't be easily taught.

After several go-rounds, late in the afternoon, I registered that he seemed defensive and angry. He certainly seemed agitated by all the clarifying questions we asked as we tried to make sense of his opinions. At that point, I finally realized, knowing quite a bit about the history of his program, that he was probably in a place of fear.

I asked him, "Are you nervous that you're going to get someone worse than applicant three, who at least you already know?"

"Yes, exactly." he replied, throwing up his hands.

"Okay," I said, "So you're afraid that whoever gets hired, regardless of who they are, regardless of their characteristics, that they'd turn out to be as challenging as - or maybe more difficult than - the new hires that didn't work out from last year?"

He exclaimed, "Yes! We cannot go back to where we were last year. We have to be better. We have to get better!"

Everyone at the table nodded and sat for a moment in quiet. We all knew these interviews were taking place months later in the year than was ideal, because of circumstances beyond anybody's control, and that part of the unnamed issue in the room had to do with how hard it was to get (and keep) good people in these kinds of jobs.

Someone on the panel spoke up and said, "We get that. Totally agree." And then they gently reiterated their concerns about applicant three. This time it seemed like he took it in, like he really heard them. I had the sense we were now more on the same page, but still frustrated because the truth was that no one felt excited about *any* of the applicants.

After a minute or so of more silence, someone spoke up with a suggestion that we interview a fourth person that wasn't able to be there that day. Everyone was amenable to that idea. We came up with a game plan as to how we could arrange a meeting with that last applicant and then reconvene for more discussion.

Over the course of the evening, I had a sense that Roy felt that somebody got him, that we did understand his concerns, and I wondered if he was thinking about all the feedback we threw around. I had always known him to be a logical thinker, and I wondered how the conversation was impacted by me and the others truly trying to let him know we cared about his program.

The next morning, we returned, and he was ready to change his mind. We interviewed the fourth person later that day - and that person was dynamite! We were ALL sold! It felt good to see how it all played out. I was so glad that there was cohesion around the decision, and that no one on our panel had the experience of being overridden.

Man to Man Empathy - Timothy Regan

In my work as healthy lifestyle counselor at a large medical clinic, people are often referred to me for weight management. One day, an African American man in his fifties walked into my office. He was well-dressed and soft-spoken. As we discussed his goals, I wondered if anything else might be going on in his life that would affect the process of losing weight.

As I began to ask about stress, I learned that this man had been through a harrowing experience just three weeks prior. In a calm voice, he described how his vehicle had been stopped by several cop cars as he began an early morning shift. He had been pulled from his seat and held face-down on the ground at gunpoint.

After some time, he was released, and in a blur, it was quickly over. Ever since, he had been having trouble sleeping and had been feeling tense and upset. He didn't, however, want to talk about things with coworkers or family members. He worried his coworkers would tease him and, as for his family, he wanted to be strong. He had seen a therapist twice, but it didn't seem to be helping.

I knew that this story was important so I sat, quietly at first, to respect his experience, and to honor that it was still affecting him deeply. Then I began, gently, to make guesses as to what it must've been like for him.

I said something like, "This really was shocking for you and maybe it's still got you shaken up a little bit. Because, as a human being, you need safety, just basic safety. With guns pointed at you, the shock can stay with you for a while."

He nodded and tentatively agreed to that. "Yeah, that's true. That makes sense," he said.

Next, I asked a little bit about respect, wondering whether the treatment he experienced offended his sense of respect. He shrugged a yes, but I didn't see much indication of a shift move through him the way that it often does when an empathy guess really lands.

I did, however, begin to feel something in my own body. There was some anger inside, maybe a little indignation. I was imagining that if I had gone through what he had it would be hard for me to sleep because I'd be mad. So, I asked him, but he definitely didn't express any anger at all. Not one iota. I was struck by that, because I'm a white male who knows that African American men are exposed to a lot of disrespect and racism in our society. It wasn't on target, though, so I circled back around to ask about the safety piece, again.

"Well," he said, "what really bothered me was

not so much about safety. I didn't think they were actually going to hurt me..."

The question prompted him to mention a new detail, though. When the policeman had a shotgun pointed at his head as he was laying there on the ground, the policeman had cocked it. In a moment of insight, my client said he believed it was this memory that had been keeping him awake, tense, and preoccupied.

I let this insight sink in and then something flashed in me, something very strong. I felt an electric heat run through me. It was like a very deep and powerful physical sensation that filled me kind of like fire; it almost made my hair stand up on end.

Suddenly, as this sensation surged through me, I felt sure I knew what the missing piece was. A word came to me, and I had to take a deep breath because tears started flowing. I said something like, "My brother, man to man, was this about dignity?"

He looked at me and tears filled his eyes. It was very uncomfortable and intense, but it was right. We sat suspended in that electric moment for several seconds. He nodded, and there was a wave of power and honor and recognition and also of togetherness. We were together in the same understanding and knowing of what dignity really was.

We sat just like that. I remember shaking my head, holding my hands open, and saying, "Yes, yes." It was three things that washed over us – recognition, acknowledgment and honoring of dignity.

As we let things settle, he seemed to shift. I simply followed him, accompanying him as his train of thought went into what he might be able to do.

I reflected to him this shift, "Now that we know what this is, dignity, you probably want to do something. Because everyone needs dignity. It's essential."

He agreed, straightening up in his chair, and then we started exploring ways he might restore that dignity, very gently. One possibility was to actually open up to his wife and receive her care and understanding. Another idea was to write a letter to the police department, to describe his experience, and maybe make a request for some form of an apology. He imagined how helpful some recognition would be for his dignity. We talked about how honoring his own voice in penning the letter, in itself, would be restoring a sense of power and agency. We left open several possible action steps as we wrapped up our conversation.

What's amazing about this story is that he came

back a week or two later and he was like a different man. He didn't even talk about the incident at first – just went on about how happy he was about the upcoming summer barbecues and family gatherings, and all the family and good food he was planning. He was positive and excited, still very humble and composed, but he was more open and playful.

It turns out, had talked to his wife and they had written the letter to the police department together. They had not sent it, but writing it was enough. He thanked me for what I did to help him move on. My attempt to be with him had truly made a difference, even though many of my guesses weren't initially on target. It was so beautiful seeing the change in him. I was inspired - It seemed like we both were.

-Timothy Regan, admin@rememberingconnection.com

Autonomy & Safety for Five-Year-Olds - Matthew Rich

I'm a Montessori teacher and was in the middle of an intricate music presentation, when I felt a little hand on my shoulder. Esetu, a five-year-old, was wanting to know whether she could use the kettle and microwave to prepare her lunch of noodle soup. She had only recently had this task presented to her, and so I requested she wait a few minutes while I finished what I was busy with so I could supervise her. I explained to her that I was concerned about her safety and would call her as soon as I became available.

However, when I got up a few minutes later to look for Esetu, I found that she had already used the kettle and that her noodles were already in the microwave... and I was quickly elevated to a point of blinding anger. *She didn't listen and do what she was told, which she should. She doesn't care about what I say. She is irresponsible. She can't be trusted.* Looking back, those thoughts appeared to be a little unreasonable, but in the heat of the moment, I swear, they seemed like objective facts. I raged silently for a bit, took some time to get in touch with what was going on underneath the anger, and then I felt more relaxed. I was ready to talk.

I approached Esetu and asked if she would be willing to let me discuss something with her. She nodded. Knowing that she was willing to talk with me now (if she wasn't, I'd be wasting time), I went on to say, "Esetu, when I ask you to wait for me to supervise you before using the kitchen equipment, and then walk in and see you using that equipment, I feel really scared because I care about you being safe from things like electrical shocks and burns. Can you tell me what you hear?"

Esetu responded by saying, "You think I'll hurt myself, BUT I know how to do it! You showed me last time, remember…"

Now, that wasn't really what I said. But I went with it and replied, "Are you frustrated, or maybe hurt, 'cos you'd like me to understand and appreciate that you can do it yourself?"

Esetu showed me a handful of fingers and said, defensively, "I'm five! And I can do it!" Then she looked down at her feet.

I asked, "Would you really like to be seen for what you can do?"

I got no response from her, so I tried again.

"So, you're telling yourself that you really can do this, but that I just won't let you? I guess it is kind of confusing and annoying to you. Would you like to know if I understand and trust what you really can do?"

Esetu looked up with tears in her eyes and nodded affirmatively.

"It really hurts when you're telling yourself I don't trust you?" I continued. "Trust is really important to you?"

At this, Esetu climbed on my knee. Her body relaxed visibly and she looked up at my face.

"Would it be okay if I told you what was going on for me, now?" I asked.

"Uh-huh," she said, still relaxed.

"I would like for you to hear that I want you to be supervised in the kitchen, not because I doubt your ability, but because I need a safe environment," I said, making eye contact. "Could you tell me what you hear me say?"

Esetu smiled and said, "You care about us? You want everybody to be safe."

The dialogue continued for a bit as we talked about sadness, and about how trust was important for us both, even though we were going about it in different ways.

Once we had everything on the table, Esetu had no further objections. She said she was willing to seek supervision before using the kettle, stove, or microwave.

A Dying Patient - Anne Walton

In the late eighties, I worked as a nurse in the hospice unit of a large hospital, which was located in an area of Vancouver that had a substantial gay population. At that time, many gay men were dying of A.I.D.S. and it was painful for the whole community. I was caring for a particular A.I.D.S. patient, a young man who was close to death, when I really learned what a simple, but profound, difference it can make when I intend to listen with my heart.

This man was in his early thirties and only a few days away from dying. While he rested on the bed, his younger brother, who couldn't have been more than twenty-five years old, was standing across the bed from me watching everything I did.

He said, "Why aren't you starting an IV for him?" "Why aren't you tube feeding him?" He seemed so focused on everything I was doing, and every word out of his mouth sounded like a demand.

At other times I might have gotten defensive but something kind of magic happened in that moment, something that I can only describe as a moment of grace.

I heard myself ask, "This must be incredibly

painful for you?"

Instantly, his whole demeanor softened, his energy totally changed, and he started to cry.

I couldn't believe how pivotal that tiny comment was! It changed our whole day together. And it was easy for me to go there as soon as I noticed I could hear what was in his heart, in addition to the words that were coming out of his mouth. That moment shifted his experience too, I believe. There was no longer a head-based focus on why I wasn't doing this or that. I hope he was able to move through the grief he was facing with a little more grace and ease.

- Anne Walton, www.chooseconnection.com

Hospital Execs - Jim Manske

My partner and I were hired by a hospital to help them with some staffing problems. The emergency room, in particular, was a mess at this hospital. They estimated over $350,000 worth of turnover costs because the nurses and the doctors weren't getting along. They reported daily drama in this work culture, and a lot of employees had quit over the course of time.

The hiring and training budgets were high, so the hospital executives wanted to find better, cheaper solutions. We gave about six hours of training to the ER staff, with some basic tools for connection and cooperation.

Over the eight months following this introductory training, the hospital's turnover costs plummeted to almost zero. So we were hired to come back and teach other classes.

One particular class was set up for the entire leadership team, including the board of directors, all senior managers, and every executive in the hospital. And attendance was required, which isn't ideal given the role "choice" plays in what we teach.

When we arrived, there was a woman in the first row who didn't look happy about being there.

Although she sat up front, which is often a good sign that there's curiosity and interest in a class, everything else about her body language said no, no, no. She held her arms crossed, her legs crossed, and sat with her body twisted away from us. And for the first part of the day, she never, ever looked at us.

I guessed that her behavior was emblematic of the culture, but rather than try to connect with her directly about not wanting to be there, we empathized—out loud—with what it's like to be in a situation in which you're telling yourself that you have to do something or else get punished. This became part of our training and weaved in well with our content on collaborating. We wanted folks to understand that whenever any of us have the idea we *have to* do something, we're actually living in what we call "jackal" consciousness, a space of life-alienating communication, and it's as if we're under the spell of threat.

My partner and I spoke to these ideas in general, and began to move through the deceptively simple process we teach around self-empathy, where people get the opportunity to transform "obligation" energy and begin connecting to their own needs.

So, as we proceeded through the exercises,

things started to shift for this woman sitting in the front row. She appeared to be following our suggestions about giving herself empathy, and as she self-empathized, it seemed like she got more connected to her motivations. Everything about her body language started to relax. And as the rest of the day wore on, not only did she shift her body language, she started engaging us with questions and challenges about our training content. It was great to see how dynamic the discussion became.

It was certainly tempting, at times, to move into education-mode, to correct some of the ideas she might've misunderstood. Instead, we just stayed with empathy, acknowledging her experience, and connecting with her by saying things such as, "So for you, it's a real concern that these communication tools will make things inefficient. Yeah. Got it."

While we were happy to answer the questions she had, we never tried to convince her of anything. We simply stayed with what was important to her when she brought up a hesitation, then went back into the material for the group.

At the end of the day, I was surprised to be treated with a warm and heartfelt hug, as she came up to offer a special goodbye.

What a transformation! We'd made a true

connection - and we had the sense that we'd offered her at least a few ideas that she would make tangible use of!

- Jim Manske, www.radicalcompassion.com

"Master" Teacher - Mary Goyer

I learned basic algebra in the eighth grade from a teacher who possessed finessed skill in working with teenagers. Everything ran well under his watch. As a kid, I took it for granted, of course. But I remember several occasions in which Mr. Beyta chose compassion in our classroom, by expertly redirecting misbehaviors without making a big deal about them. He was a math guy, obviously—not a "warm and fuzzy" type—yet we all knew he cared. As I look back on a particular memory, I realize just how much empathy I received from Mr. Beyta one day, even though it took me years for me to recognize it.

I remember sitting in his class, gazing out the window one afternoon. It was after lunch, I was a little spacey, and I didn't realize I'd said, "Those clouds are massive," out loud until the whole room turned to look at me.

"Goyer," he said, heaving his chest in a sigh, "attention up here, okay?"

I was startled back into the room. But since I had already disrupted things, without exactly meaning to, I impulsively decided to move forward with a simple question that shot into my head, one that'd been in the back of my mind for weeks.

"Okay, but real quick. Why do the kids call you Master Beyta?" I asked. It was a nickname I'd heard my friends use several times and I wanted to understand the context, not realizing at all that it was a sexual reference.

He stopped. He tilted his head. And he looked at me, blinking, for several seconds. I had no consciousness of having suddenly entered us both into delicate territory. I was aware that I was pushing it by asking a non-math question after interrupting the class already. But I wanted to know!

Master Beyta. Was he a black-belt in karate, maybe? Was it a religious thing? A quick answer would've satisfied my curiosity.

I could see the wheels in his head turning, as he calculated possible responses. Now I know, looking back, he must've been assessing the sincerity behind my question (smart-ass or naïve?), the answer to which would direct him down very different branches of a decision tree.

The fact that he was taking such a long time, though, was baffling to me that afternoon. I thought, impatiently, "Just tell me."

He didn't. In fact, he didn't say anything at all for a while. Instead, he slowly scanned the room, took another big breath, and said in an even voice,

"Can somebody help Mary answer her question after class, please?"

And then, without skipping another beat, he turned back to the chalkboard and launched into the day's lesson.

I threw my hands up in a little gesture of frustration, but once we moved on I forgot about it, completely. It seemed everyone else did, too; no one mentioned the conversation as we left class.

I went on after that year to a different high school than most of my friends, but ran into a group of them at a play when I was a senior. We hugged and said our hellos. One of them, who'd taken that class with me, suddenly burst out laughing and said, "Oh my gosh, you all, you wouldn't believe the time Mary asked Mr. Beyta, right in the middle of him teaching, why all the kids called him 'masturbate-a' as if it was nothing."

I winced. Wait... what? I did WHAT?

Then the dawn of realization began to wash over me. Oh, no. No, no. The memory registered, I saw the whole scene unfold through a new pair of eyes, and everyone laughed as I shuddered in misery. I couldn't stop shaking my head.

"Masturbate-a", not "Master Beyta"! No, no, no. I was nauseous. The other kids must've thought I was being mischievous in bringing up the nickname to his face. Oh, my God. If he'd been triggered, he could've easily punished me, or leveled me with any number of sarcastic responses, exposing my naïveté.

I didn't even know I was in a minefield of possible humiliations that day, yet, I made it out self-esteem intact. Mr. Beyta's grounded (and elegant!) response may not have been consciously oriented around empathy in the moment he said what he did, but it was, nonetheless, exactly the type of empathy-in-action that my tender teenage soul needed.

- Mary Goyer, www.consciouscommunication.co

Disdain From My Research Supervisor - Hema Pokharna

Upon completion of my Ph.D. program, I received a postdoctoral fellowship at Case Western Reserve University. By then, I had a certain light-hearted attitude towards life and research. I was to work on a research hypothesis which I had designed as a graduate student. I was very excited about the project. With good fortune, I was in a position to collaborate with a skillful biochemist and an excellent researcher whose guidance I very much wanted.

Yet, in one of our early discussions, he was so frustrated with me that he said, "Are you sure you have a Ph.D., Hema? You don't seem to be bright."

I felt very sad and scared because I was considered to be a good scientist and productive researcher, so far. My identity was in jeopardy. In that moment, I considered myself a failure since he was a very renowned scientist; his words were the truth to me. This was a very painful experience.

After spending three hours of crying and breathing, I returned to his office renewed with compassion and said, "Can I spend a few moments in your luminous presence so that I can brighten myself?"

By then, I think he was aware of what had

happened and was very kind to me ever after.

Particularly rewarding at this time was the fact that I remembered to breathe. At this point, I found and understood that the best antidote to any violence was the breath. This has been one of the most exciting and major turning points in my development. Toward the end of the fellowship, we had published three papers together. And my continued association with him has meant a great deal to me. After that day, my "Ph.D." stood for "Psychologically healthy and Delightful".

The time I spent breathing and crying was the time I allowed myself to stop and get the benefit of experiencing and reacting with freshness, taking time to remove any prejudice and restriction. This, to me, was meditation in its own form.

In those three hours of breathing, I was aware of the suffering caused by unmindful speech and inability to listen to others. I affirmed my own convictions to cultivate loving speech and deep listening in order to bring joy and happiness to my fellow beings and relieve them of their suffering, if possible. After understanding that words can create happiness or suffering, I am now much more conscious to learn ways to speak truthfully, with words that inspire self-confidence, joy, and hope.

- *Hema Pokharna, www.doctorsbeyondstress.com*

Saving Personnel During Budget Cuts - Dian Killian

In many large business organizations, internal teams and departments can either "hire" other departments in-house for work needed, often getting the best possible price for those contracts, or they can outsource the work, if there's a good reason to do so. It all depends on the discretion of the budgeting department, who acts as the main intermediary while one team makes a bid to another team, negotiating to work together rather than hire help from the outside.

I was working in one such company with a senior executive, who was in the middle of a bidding process, trying to get his team hired for an internal project. He was very focused, as the head of his department, on keeping the contract in-house. It was one that could have potentially been outsourced, but he wanted it for his own team so they could show what they were capable of, so they could have the satisfaction of further growing the company, and certainly so that they would all remain employed.

It looked as if his team had been hired, so they excitedly began planning out the project when he found out that the budget had been cut. The project was a no-go. Frustrated and disappointed, since he had already planned on his team having the income as well as the work, he was furious because he believed there was a personality issue behind the cut-back decision.

When he came to me for coaching, I started by just listening to his story. Once he'd had the chance to talk, without any focus on action steps, a fascinating thing came out of the conversation. He effortlessly set aside all his frustration about the office politics, and got clear that his main priority was really quite simple: the budget.

Would he have the funds to retain his staff? That's the main thing he cared about.

With this focus, he knew he wanted a valid project to keep his team engaged so he wouldn't have to lay anyone off. We talked both about his goal of keeping all his workers employed, and about what him standing up for his team meant for the company as a whole, values-wise.

As we spoke, he was also able to empathically connect with the person who controlled the budget, and what must've been going on for them in terms of integrity when they broke the news to him about the cut. He touched into the pressures that exist politically for the budgeting department, and particularly connected - mentally, at least - with the person who'd made the top-down budgetary decision at hand.

Suddenly, two completely different strategies came to him, neither of which had occurred to him before. First, he wanted to approach the budget-decider and listen empathically to them to make sure he really did understand the constraints they felt they were under. And then, if there was room on their end to entertain a creative solution, he had a renegotiation in mind.

"I understand," he said when he had a chance to begin the conversation with them, "that you were asked to cut a certain amount from the budget at large, and that you did it from a number of different departments. Is that true?"

"Yes, that's it."

"And so you feel that you can't give us the money that we'd hoped for anymore, right?"

"Right."

"Okay, well I have a completely different idea that would be good for the company and keep my team intact, working on something really important. Are you open to hearing it?"

The person was open, and nodded their head.

He said, "This company is committed to spending a certain amount of money on public service advocacy. I have a project in mind that would cost about X amount and is in line with our values here." (Coincidentally, the amount was about the same as the amount of money cut from the team budget.)

He then went on to outline an education-based outreach project in Africa that would focus on hygienic treatment of bottled milk products. He had the data on what it would involve, the number of lives saved, etc. And then he wrapped up with a few more statistics to reflect the way the pitch was in alignment with the company's social mission.

Long story short, a connection was made and the budget request for this service project was ultimately approved. My client's team - all of it - had the resources they needed to work on something incredibly meaningful to them, far more satisfying than the original project would have been. And his relationship with his colleague in the budgeting department was restored.

He was so happy, saying things never would have unfolded so well if, during our conversation, he hadn't cleared through his resentment to get reoriented around his core needs, which essentially boiled down to relationships and collaboration.

- Dian Killian, www.workcollaboratively.com

Apologizing to My Students - Kevin Goyer

I teach high school special education on an alternative campus, in a program designed to help students get back on track academically after excessive absences from school. It's not unusual for the kids I work with to suffer from anxiety and depression, so I've learned a lot about empathy and connection from these teens.

I remember one instance in which I was working with two girls who were upset with me, and I shocked them by doing something out of the ordinary from their perspective. I apologized to them.

I had initially asked them to use diligence and work during a set amount of time on a math assignment, which I assumed would be plenty of time to complete it. I essentially said, "Do your work, then you'll get some free time today."

When I checked back, they hadn't finished the work, so I took away that opportunity for free time. They were angry, and although I was confused as to why they thought my expectation was unreasonable, I decided to sit down and have a chat with them to try and understand their perspective.

They thought I was asking for them to simply stay busy and make progress during the timeframe;

they didn't realize I meant I anticipated them completing a specific set of work. So when the consequence came in, to them, it seemed unfair.

I took a breath. It can be so frustrating to watch students not step into what they seem fully capable of accomplishing, and I needed a moment with my exasperation.

I didn't change my mind about them losing their free time. But I did apologize for wording my expectation in the way that I did. I said that I wish I'd have been crystal clear in my directions during class so we'd at least have started on the same page.

Neither of them said much, but I noticed their body language changed, softened, when I acknowledged that we seemed to have interpreted what I said differently.

After that had happened, I asked, "Have you ever had an adult or a teacher apologize to you for making a mistake?"

"No, never." they replied, clearly still surprised.

It was helpful in repairing the situation and, I hope, in reminding them that I care about their needs and perspectives even when I hold a different point of view. And, since that conversation, I've made a point to model for all my classes how to handle the inevitability of making mistakes.

Empathy in the Community: Caring for Strangers

Car, the Clubs, and the Cab Driver - Thom Bond

A few years back, when I was living in Manhattan, I loaned my car, a station wagon, to a friend who needed it to move into her new apartment. We had agreed that she would return it early that evening. I waited and waited, and waited some more. No call, no car. I drifted to sleep waiting on my couch.

At about 2:30 in the morning, I was awakened by a phone call. "Thom, I just finished moving and I just don't have the energy to return the car tonight."

I inquired, "Where did you leave it?"

She informed me that it was parked on a street in the meat-packing district (a less-than-safe part of town) with my golf clubs in plain sight in the back. Ten minutes later, after some serious self-empathy work (that's a story for another time), I was headed to rescue my car and my precious toys.

I staggered out into the night and eventually found a cab. I climbed in and we headed along the edge of Manhattan Island down the West Side Highway to my car and my clubs. As we drove alongside the Hudson River, we passed the USS Intrepid, a decommissioned battleship that functions as a floating museum.

From the back seat, I could see only the cab driver's eyes reflected in the rearview mirror. He spoke. "The last time I saw that ship, I was stationed in Viet Nam."

We made eye contact in the mirror. I replied, "That must bring up quite a bit for you."

"It does."

I listened into the silence that followed. More eye contact, more space. After a time, he spoke again. "When we came back, everybody hated us."

We sat quietly as the tires thumped rhythmically on the seams of the road, sounding eerily like a beating heart. We just sat there, making space for his pain, his need for being seen, for appreciation, for love. I watched the pain slowly seep into his occasional glance.

I spoke. "I imagine that was tough, risking your life like that. I bet it would have made a big difference to have gotten even *some* appreciation."

"Yes... Yes, it would have."

Still seeing only his eyes in the mirror, I watched as the tears slowly filled his eyes. We continued our ride, without speaking a word, as we rolled through the empty streets to our destination.

A few minutes later we arrived. I reached through the little glass hatch and paid the fare... and with compassion and connection in my heart said a simple "thank you." I swung the door open and started on my way. From behind me, I heard the sound of the cab door opening.

As I turned, there was my new found friend, with an outstretched hand and a look of pure relief in his eyes, walking toward me. "Thank *you*." We shook hands and parted.

- *Thom Bond,* www.compassioncourse.org

Heckling Baseball Fans - Becka Kelley

Going to a baseball game was not my first choice for a Saturday activity. Even though I started off with a questionable attitude, I found that I was enjoying myself, until about a quarter of the way through the game when a group of guys came in and started shouting obscenities at the players. They were saying stuff that was really hard for me to hear like, "What a fag! Get some balls!" and "You suck, Smith!"

You get the idea.

The group of guys laughed and egged each other on, although one of them was doing most of the shouting.

It was so painful and disturbing to hear their comments that I told my boyfriend I might want to leave. But then I had an idea: maybe I could talk to them and ask them to stop making those obscene and offensive comments. A lot of fear came up in me as I had this thought. I sat with it a while, took a few breaths, gathered my courage, and I went over to go have a talk with them. I walked right up to the guy who was the noisiest, offered my hand to shake, and said, "Hi, I'm Becka."

First, he looked confused, then proud. He puffed his chest out, glanced around at the other guys, then faced me again with a charming smile. I'm pretty sure he thought I was hitting on him.

I hadn't figured out what to say, yet, so I began by asking how he was and whether he was enjoying the game. Then, I said, "I came over because I heard you guys shouting things to the players out there and I'm curious about it. Why do you do that?"

He replied, saying, "Oh, they don't mind. This is how it always is. It encourages them. We always do this to each other." I realized he was actually shouting comments to people he knew and regularly played games with.

I responded with, "Oh, so this is how you guys connect and kind of show your support for each other?"

"Yeah," he replied.

I said something like, "Wow, that's so interesting. You know, when I heard your comments, that's not what I thought. I would have thought you hated them. I know if I were out there hearing that stuff coming my way, I would be really hurt. It would be hard to even hear those things."

He said, "Ah, yeah, well you're probably just sensitive. We can handle it. We always do this with each other."

At this point, I had a realization. I wasn't going to ask them to stop making comments. My intention had shifted from trying to change their behavior to wanting to understand their perspective. I felt my body loosen as I let go of my judgment and agenda. Instead, I was experiencing openness and curiosity. I still disagreed with their choice to motivate their teammates using shame, but I was able to let go of labeling them "wrong" or "bad" people.

I never did ask for the heckling to stop, as I'd originally intended. Mostly because I just didn't think it would work. But also because I had a sense of satisfaction just for being brave enough to talk and connect with them. That seemed like a big enough accomplishment for one day. I figured that when the yelling started back up - which I assumed it would - I'd leave the game without feeling quite so angry and judgmental.

Interestingly, after I left, they stayed quiet. They stopped the heckling on their own! It was crazy! I didn't know whether it was because of me or not, but they ended up leaving the stands shortly after our conversation ended.

I'm so proud of the courage and vulnerability I practiced that day. I had the guts to go and talk to a group of guys I was pretty intimidated by about something that was really affecting me. I was able to connect and develop some understanding with this group of people I had vilified. It was a very empowering and compassion-building experience that has continued to stay with me.

- Becka Kelley, www.beckakelley.com

Furious Neighbours - Manuela Santiago-Teigeler

Last week, I walked out of my house and saw two strange men fighting with each other on my block. One looked visibly upset, was screaming, and pretended to kick the other man's grey car. The car owner had his hands full with moving boxes and was threatening to call the police.

I felt a bit anxious about the violence I was witnessing and even worried for my own safety while I watched the scene unfold. The man with the car was getting pretty frustrated, and I could sense his overwhelm. The first man, still ranting, spit on the grey car. But I sensed he was not really a threat to me. Just *angry*.

I walked right up to the man who was screaming and said loudly, "You look ANGRY!"

He then turned his attention to me, away from the grey car and its owner, and proceeded to tell me, loudly, how his pants got sprinkled when the driver drove past and splashed a puddle.

I continued by saying, "That must be frustrating!"

He began to walk away from the other man to tell me just how frustrating it was. As he spoke, I noticed he began to lower his voice.

The car owner looked at me with relief and turned back to his moving boxes, happy to get out of dealing with a mad stranger.

As for the first man, I simply looked him in the eye and listened to his pain, while we slowly started walking away together. I learned as he spoke that he was very poor, that he had just paid to wash his pants, and could not afford to wash his pants at the laundromat again. He totally calmed down as I listened, and when we got to his house he wished me a good day.

It was not easy, but I am glad I stopped to help these men. This situation could have spiraled with the involvement of police, tickets, court dates, anger, physical violence, etc. I'm glad it didn't turn into a vicious cycle of pain.

Intensity and Diversity - Timothy Regan

As an NVC (Non-Violent Communication) trainee, I attended an NVC intensive workshop led by its founder, the late Dr. Marshall Rosenberg. In this body of work, there's a huge value around shared power, so in this way our workshop strayed from typical ones in which the leader is basically in charge and totally deferred to. It was established explicitly that everyone present was responsible for creating the learning container, cultivating safety for each other, and expressing their own needs.

We, as a group, had moved through that first phase of getting to know each other, often characterized by cautious hesitation. We felt pretty comfortable with one another and had gotten to that deeper level of community in which self-disclosure, risk, and unguarded emotions really surface.

As we started one morning, a Native American woman began opening up about some stories of deep, deep chaos and heartbreak in her family and community. She kept speaking with more emotional intensity and with increasingly graphic details of things that she had experienced that broke her heart. It wasn't the first time she'd shared like this. Repeatedly, since we'd arrived, she'd taken up a lot of space in the group with stories of searing pain. And it never seemed to let up or help her in any obvious way. People had tried to give her empathy but it was never clear that it landed.

We all know this person in groups, who gets labeled as: needy, disturbed, inconsiderate, and sometimes scary. All these labels were up, there was pressure in the room, and there were two options. Suppress it and keep listening, or express the frustration. And that's what ended up happening.

There was a priest in our group. After ten long minutes of her talking passed, the priest stood up, stomped his foot, and said, "Will you shut the fuck up?"

There was a shock and a silence in the room, but there also a sense of relief. She was shocked into silence while he said a few more words. Marshall just sat, watching this happen. He didn't jump in or anything at all.

Then, a woman stood up for the first woman, and said to the priest, "How dare you attack her and slam her like that when she's trying to get some help? That's the most rude, inconsiderate thing I've ever seen. How dare you?"

She was angry and blamed the priest, who now stood quietly.

Then, another young man, who we'd learned

was interested in social justice, suddenly spoke up to her. He jumped up and said, also sounding angry, "Well, let's start with the priest because obviously he was feeling something strong. Let's actually hear from him. Don't shut him down. Don't do that."

I looked around the room at the four figures now standing, the woman who first spoke, the priest, the second woman, and the young man. Other hands were shooting up in the room. It looked like things were going to turn into a big mess very quickly.

Marshall, the facilitator, stepped in at this point and did three things. He asked the young man to pause, he acknowledged all the people who wanted to speak, and he noted the tension that was building up in the room again.

He then asked the young man if he could say something to him. I think Marshall offered the young man an empathy guess along these lines, "Are you feeling a deep sense of frustration and maybe even some hopelessness as you speak, because you're so wanting acknowledgement and people to express themselves fully and really be heard with acknowledgement? Is that it?"

The young man said, "Yes! That's what I'm trying to get, thank you."

Then Marshall replied, "I've got a little

possibility for you. Would you be interested?"

When the young man nodded yes, Marshall said, "Might you want to guess about the woman who spoke before you, what her needs are, why she was speaking, and where the energy was coming from in her voice? Maybe guess her feelings and her needs?"

The man nodded again and said, "Oh, okay. Yeah, I'm willing to try that."

So he looked at her and asked if she was really scared when the priest stood up. Had it reminded her of her own family and now she really wanted to take a stand? He asked if it had taken a lot of courage for her to stand up.

As he spoke, we watched her calm immediately and visibly relax. He went on to ask if she really wanted to protect the first woman. To have safety, dignity, and inclusion for everybody.

She began to brim up with tears as she nodded her head yes.

The whole group paused and watched as she processed waves of emotion after that acknowledgement. After several minutes, she took a breath and spontaneously turned to the priest.

She said, "Listen, I'm sorry I yelled at you. I can see now that you were probably feeling frustrated because you wanted everyone to be able to participate. You wanted a deep sense of inclusion and understanding with everybody having space to express themselves. Is that it?"

The priest, who was now sitting, also began to relax and open up. He began talking about where he works and all the trauma that he sees on a daily basis. He went into the workshop carrying a lot of heartbreak and said he couldn't take any more. He was wanting relief and some help for that.

So, the group gave him more air time for his heartbreak and trauma. We probably only spent fifteen or so minutes listening to him, but his grief began to shift noticeably. He felt like his needs were honored.

At this point, the priest turned to the original Native American woman who had been so vocal about her struggles and he apologized to her. He expressed regret about the effect he might have had on her when he spoke up to her so suddenly.

She replied back, "I'm touched but, well, it didn't bother me too much. I appreciate you standing up."

It turned out, after all that, she was okay with it! But the whole room changed because of the empathy that flowed from one direction to the other. Just one drop of empathy that Marshall gave to the young man, reversed the escalating string of anger, frustration, and blame.

-Timothy Regan, admin@rememberingconnection.com

A Prisoner's Insight - Mair Alight

I was running a class with a group of men in San Quentin prison who were talking one day about one man's ongoing conflict on the yard. He said something about needing to "stand up for himself" to be respected, the implications of that phrase lost on nobody.

In response, another guy in the class, an old-timer, nodded listening, then said to his classmate, "I'd do it differently."

"Okay, how?" the first man asked.

The old-timer replied, "I'd give the other guy the moment."

I listened, fascinated, and jumped in asking, "Wow, what does that mean? What does 'give him the moment' mean?"

He said, "Well, when you see someone and you see he's all twisted up, something's happened, he's not in his right state. You know, just back away, just give him the moment."

I said, "Oh, this is what I call empathy in action."

"What are you talking about?" they all asked. To them, empathy was all about what you do or say. It hadn't occurred to them that *not* doing something could be empathy, too.

I told them, "It sounds like you've tried this but just had a different name for it. You've figured out, by watching someone's body language and gestures when they're activated, that something's not working for them. So, when you 'gave them the moment' to just let them be without engaging, trying to correct, or anything else... that was empathy. 'Giving him the moment' was empathy."

That day, they learned that empathy doesn't need to be about words at all. And I learned, or rather was reminded, just how much better the world would be if we all had the space to give someone else the moment a little more often.

- Mair Alight, www.Mair@MairAlight.com

From Self-Loathing to Self-Acceptance in Ten Minutes - Katherine Revoir

At a four-day healing seminar, a fellow participant had paid to have a session of personal, intensive work done, supported by the whole group. I offered to record her work with my phone so she wouldn't have to worry about trying to take notes about the process. I was really happy to contribute in this way because her session was quite involved, lasted at least an hour, and I figured she'd be glad to have a recording to reference later.

After her time ended, and I was satisfied that I'd captured a lot of valuable stuff for her, I looked at the screen, saw the word "done" and hit a little red button that swiftly erased the entire hour's recording.

In denial, I grabbed a techie friend and asked, "OK, now what did I do wrong with this recording?"

She replied, "Well, there's no recording here."

I said, "No, no, no. I must have done something wrong. It must be saved somewhere. I could not have possibly done that."

She looked again and repeated, "There's no recording here. I'm sorry."

I was in shock and I felt my stomach tighten.

My chest clenched and a heavy sensation of shame began to pour over me, like a can of paint was dumped over my head.

Before I knew it, familiar thoughts started circling in. How could you have done this? You know you're no good at this stuff. How could you let this happen? Why didn't you just ask somebody else to help you? These self-berating phrases wouldn't stop. And as it dawned on me that the recording had definitely been erased, I started to cry in spite of myself.

Another participant, Maria, saw my tears and asked if I'd like support. I was still half in shock, half in denial, with grief and shame mixed in. So, she started talking in a very calm tone, which helped me breathe.

"Are you kind of panicked?"

"Yeah, I am." I replied. "My throat is all closed up and my body is shaking."

"And scared?"

"Yeah, kind of! I'm feeling scared because I can't believe that I would have done that, that I would be capable of blowing it so badly."

My new friend had paid a pretty penny for her process. The work was complicated enough that everyone else who went through a paid session had taken pages of notes by hand. And now my friend would have nothing.

Maria asked, "Did you really want to be helpful?"

Yes! It seemed obvious. Yeah, of course. Of course I'm upset! Of course I'm feeling shame. I'm crying!

Still, it was better than sitting alone in self-criticism. The company was good but the shame continued to spiral. Maria sat through all of it, listened, and every so often asked more questions. What else was up for me? What else was I needing? Oh, so many things. To be competent in technology was important; my need to contribute; wanting to see myself as somebody that had confidence in figuring things like this out in the future.

The negative voices were deafening. You're never going to be able to do something like this again. You can't be trusted. All of the old, old childhood blaming, self-shaming memes were right there. But my body had relaxed some.

Then, I noticed that the woman I'd "let down," the friend who didn't know about any of this yet, was sitting close by. I realized I had to confess right away.

I grabbed a chair next to her, crying still, and

said, "Oh my God, I can't believe what I just did. It was so important to me to make this recording for you and it didn't work. It didn't happen. I recorded over it and I'm just so sorry."

I could barely talk, I was crying so hard. She just looked at me and had so much love in her eyes.

She said, "Oh well. Those things happen."

I couldn't believe it. She wasn't getting what a horrible, awful thing I'd done. She wasn't understanding how badly I'd screwed up. She was so loving and... unconcerned! I was stunned. I repeated myself in case she hadn't grasped my point.

Then, she spoke again. "Actually, what's really moving me right now is how much you cared, how important this was to you."

We talked a bit more, hugged, and after I had a chance to recover, I noticed something pretty incredible. The previous shame, only some of which was about the actual incident, had totally drifted away. I kept opening the closet of my mind expecting the ghosts and those old skeletons to be there as time went on... but they were gone. No perseverating for weeks. Nothing. Those self-criticisms just left. For me, receiving this empathy left me so calm and relaxed, it was almost like I was in a lounge chair under an umbrella on a tropical beach, listening to the gentle sound of ocean waves.

- Katherine Revoir, www.RicherLiving.org/Counseling

Zeke and the KKK - Catherine Cadden

Sixteen-year-old Zeke was an active member of the Ku Klux Klan. I met him when I had the opportunity to work with some high schoolers in the San Francisco Bay Area, teaching a two-day workshop on nonviolence. The first day was focused on how to transcend fixed ideas and perceptions of others while considering their human needs. On the second day, we worked primarily on conflict resolution skills, but we also really wanted to support the connections between students.

Zeke was uncomfortable with all of this, and by day two, he had sat with his discomfort long enough. In a room full of people he saw as Jewish, Gay, Black, Liberal, the wrong kind of White, and Female, he had trouble keeping quiet. When it was revealed that a Jewish girl's sister was getting married to another woman, he couldn't help but to say what was on his mind.

"That's just wrong!" he exclaimed.

"Are you uncomfortable because there are people in here you're not used to connecting with?" I asked.

In response, Zeke explained his beliefs about why certain people are simply "born inferior." After this monologue, that stimulated agitation in several people throughout the room, he added a bit more.

"Well, you know, I hate these people but don't get me wrong. I'm not a violent person. I wouldn't want harm to come to them. It's just I hate certain people."

"Hmm." I replied. "Now I'm confused, because you're saying you hate these people yet you don't want any harm to come to them. I am guessing you might even have some confusion about your feelings towards these people. Because you say you don't want to be violent, yet you speak of hate."

Zeke continued to listen with his arms folded across his chest, his eyes fixed on mine.

I continued, "And I'm also confused about your choice to be a member of the KKK. From what I know, they have created an amazing amount of violence against the folks you say you hate. Can you tell me why you're a member? What was your primary motivation to join?"

Zeke looked right into me, and said, "My dad is a member of the KKK!"

The room bristled with comments. One student, Terrance, chimed in, "Ah man, just 'cuz your Dad's a hater doesn't mean you gotta be one, too!"

Nodding to that profound statement, I looked

into Zeke's eyes as intensely as he had looked into mine and reflected, "I'm actually hearing how much you'd like to connect to your dad. I am also hearing that maybe you feel conflicted about being a member of an organization that tries to create connection through violence and hating others."

Leaning toward Zeke, trying to tangibly soften the room with my presence, I asked, "Has this really met your need to connect with your father?"

"Yeah, I guess I joined 'cuz I hoped to get closer to my dad. I just wanted to get along with him," he replied, looking a little unsteady.

Zeke's eyes swelled with water but he was not going to cry, not in front of this group. He paused, breathed a full inhale followed by a very audible exhale, as if he was trying to regain his composure. I wasn't sure if he was impacted by the gravity of this new awareness or if he merely wanted to hold back his tears.

It didn't matter. The wheels were already in motion.

When Zeke sat for a little longer in this empathic connection, which afforded him the opportunity to link up his mind with his heart, he realized that he had not joined the KKK because he hated certain people. Rather, he was desperate to find a way to connect with his father.

We carried on with the day, but he walked up to me after the workshop and said, "You know, that was the first time I felt fear begin to leave my body. I'm actually relieved."

With his new clarity, he began to assess the effectiveness of his choice, and decided that hating others was truly not his path, not an expression of his authentic presence. He was able to get past the enemy images his mind had created about some of these other people - and the fixed ideas he had about himself - to see what he really needed. Zeke ultimately decided to quit the KKK. He developed new friendships. And he continued to work on various other strategies to find a connection with his dad.

- Catherine Cadden, www.playinthewild.org

Antidote to Road Rage - Mark Schultz

One Saturday, I was driving home along a very busy two-lane highway in Arizona when a motorcycle pulled onto the road directly in from me. It was a dirt bike and the rider was dressed in full racing leathers and helmet. He was driving well below the speed limit, so I came up behind him and followed him into town. Suddenly, he slowed down to a crawl, traveling about 5 miles an hour, so I slowed, too.

Meanwhile, the traffic began to back up a long way behind me. As we approached the first signal light entering the town, the motorcyclist pulled over but as I drove by to pass, he pulled behind me and began to follow me. Closely and purposefully.

I was worried because I began thinking the motorcyclist was angry at me, perhaps for following him closer than he liked, and I didn't know what he might do. I was afraid to pull over because of the potential for physical violence. But I decided that I would stop in the road near a lot of people, hoping that having witnesses in the vicinity might change the context of our upcoming encounter.

So I found a good place and stopped. The motorcyclist immediately got off his bike and quickly approached my vehicle. I rolled the window down and he began yelling at me, exclaiming he was going to pull me out of the car and beat me. I was terrified. I took a breath, and spoke energetically, "I get it, you're really mad. You want to be safe out there on the road."

He stopped in its tracks. He took a step back, as the words clearly touched him. He wasn't expecting to be heard. At that moment, the entire situation shifted.

He said, "That's right. I do want to be safe."

He spoke on for a moment or two and then left. No fists were thrown and as I watched him drive away, I took a huge sigh of relief. Genuine empathy is a powerful thing.

- Mark Schultz, www.nvcacademy.com

Surviving Gun Point - Srinath Waidler-Barker

In 2012, I was invited to be a supporter in the kitchen at a four-day Sun Dance in Chacon, New Mexico. At the time, I lived a simple life, as a wandering spiritual seeker, possessing only what could be carried on my own back. I had no car to get to the Lakota Sun Dance, so I waited on the side of the road to try to get a ride from one of the town neighbors, to go to the dance in this very rural village in the poorest county in the United States, Mora County, New Mexico.

It was raining, so I sang songs to the beloved divine energy of the Universe while I waited to persist in my practice of Thinking Restoratively to See Restoratively.

After about 25 minutes of prayerful singing, a man stopped to pick me up. In order to avoid getting further soaked by the downpour, I swiftly jumped into the cab of the truck and sat the two bags down by my feet on the floor.

He asked me where I was going.

"Chacon," I said.

"I am going to Mora. I can take you that far, then you have another 7 miles to go," he said.

"Okay, thanks. Yes, I know, I used to live in

Cleveland, down the road from Mora," I said.

As I settled in and buckled up in the dry truck cab, I looked over and saw that the man in the driver's seat had a gun pointed at me.

I was surprised at how calm I felt, seeing the gun. I remained detached and calm, and thought to myself, "This must be a fear of death test from my Meditation Master. If this body is going to die right now, I (the Soul) might as well Think and See Restoratively and concentrate my mind on the Beloved Divine Energy of the Universe within this man, seeing him as my own Mother, so I will go to the abode of Eternal Joy if this body is meant to perish.

I might as well offer some selfless service, and be an instrument for this man to receive some compassionate listening and empathy on the way, because he must be in pain if he is holding up a gun.

I quickly moved my prayer mala beads from my wrist and gently, quietly, and subtly placed my right hand on my right knee. I pointed them towards the driver so that they mirrored the aim of the gun.

I sat back, relaxed, and concentrated my mind on seeing the man as my own Mother. Focusing on the beloved divine energy in him, I said something using the language of the heart, called Compassionate Communication.

I said to the man, "I see you are holding a gun towards me on the seat. Are you feeling concerned and needing safety and protection?"

The man said, "Yes. I want to be generous and give people rides around here, but I am afraid of drug addicts who might want to stab me with heroine needles and steal money to buy drugs and alcohol." He went on about all the violence he was facing in the village.

He told me about the turbulence going on with his neighbors and his own family as we drove down the two-lane highway close to where I used to live in Hummingbird Community, studying the art of Conscious Co-Creation.

I listened quietly, and persisted in trying to see the man as my own Mother, clicking my mala prayer beads as loudly as I could while I had my mantra aimed at him. It helped me stay alert, compassionate, courageous, and in touch with the truth that Beloved Divine Energy in the Soul is eternal.

After several minutes, I responded and guessed, "You must be torn in two because you want to be generous and serve travelers that pass through the community. Yet, you are also nervous about safety and concerned about increasing substance abuse violence. You really want there to be peace, security, and harmony here in Mora County? Is that it?"

The man said, "Yeah, that's totally it."

He went into detail about further violence going on in the village of Mora. I listened for about another ten minutes, with the gun still pointed at me, loudly clicking my prayer beads one mantra at a time as I focused on the Beloved Divine Energy flowing through the man - rather than our differences.

When the man finished sharing about a violent family feud, I wondered out loud, "So you sound very upset about alcohol and drug violence going on between your relatives and want to see more safety, compassion, and justice here in this rural village area? Is that it?"

"Yes," said the man. Then he asked, "So what do you do Srinath?"

"Well, I live with what possessions I can carry on my own back. I practice selfless service and meditation, mostly working on Racial Justice, building Restorative Systems, learning to host Restorative Circles, and serving Mother Earth. And I offer Holistic Empathy in villages, small communities, and schools. And I want to work in youth jails to share meditation."

I continued, "Now, I am going on a spiritual pilgrimage to a Lakota Sun Dance to support and serve my Aunty Pat, who is dancing, and also my sister, Lyla, who is praying in the Women's Moon Circle Tent. I'm planning to try to lend a hand wherever it's needed in the kitchen."

The man's eyes expressed an interested desire to hear more so I went on a little further still hanging on tightly to my prayer mala.

"My spiritual Mother has embraced over 35,000,000 people, and She considers each and every human being to be Her own child. She tirelessly offers humanitarian and community building projects to feed the homeless on the streets through Mother's Kitchen, shares Integrated Amrita Meditation with youth in prisons, supports Indigenous communities in villages in India, and supports disaster relief projects like donating a million dollars to embrace the devastation after Hurricane Katrina."

The man said, "Hearing all this, I don't think I need this gun out anymore."

And he put it away in the glove box. "In fact, I'd like to drive you 14 miles out of my way, all the way to Chacon, to support you to do your selfless service at this Lakota Sun Dance."

I calmly said, "Thanks."

In this way, both the man and myself ended up transforming gun violence, together. Together, we contributed to at least one day on Earth where no one was admitted to the hospital due to violence.

May all the beings in all the worlds be peaceful and happy.

Feeling Out of Place - Edwin Rutsch

I attended a professional training focused on new education models along with about twenty-five other people. We were doing a lot of experiential work in groups, but some of the instructions were unclear. In fact, for one of the activities, the facilitator gave us a very muddled task that had to do with somehow expressing the nature of education.

The man next to me raised his hand saying he didn't really understand what was being asked of the group.

The facilitator repeated the instructions, "Do this, do that, then that…" and it still didn't quite make sense to me. He was trying to explain and explain, but somehow it just wasn't coming across.

I didn't get the sense that the man asking for help felt any clearer than I did. Usually in these kinds of situations when I'm not really understanding an activity, I just go rogue and do whatever seems fun or relevant to me. But when I looked over at the guy next to me, I could just see the frustration and tension written all over him.

He was shaking his head a little and seemed stressed. So after we were told to get started, I began to empathize with him, rather than try to figure out what we were supposed to do.

I said, "I can see that you're really stressed, is that right?"

"Yeah!" he replied. "I'm totally overwhelmed and confused about what to do."

I reflected back his words. "Oh, okay, you're overwhelmed, confused - you don't know what's going on here."

He nodded, yes.

I asked, "Is there more?"

He replied that he felt alienated in the room and ready to leave. He went on to say he felt excluded and like he didn't really belong. And he repeated that he was seconds from walking out.

"Wow!" I exclaimed. "You're ready to walk out!"

"Yeah. I feel really disconnected in here," he said. "These people aren't my people. They're progressives. They're all white; I'm not. They have a certain mentality. I don't belong here."

So I just said back, "Okay, so you're disconnected because it seems like the people aren't your kind of people here."

He said, "Yeah, I'm feeling all this anxiety here. It's really making me sad. Actually, I feel downright resentful of these people. I'm pretty irritated!"

I basically kept reflecting back my understanding of what he was saying. But it seemed to work for him. He kept nodding his head and

After several minutes of this, he took a breath and said in a calmer voice, "I do realize that part of this is my own story that these people here are so different from me. Maybe I'm just telling myself this, and in actually I'm sitting here judging the folks around me."

I reflected that then asked, "Well, what are you needing here, do you think?"

And he began to talk again.

Now, meanwhile, our whole table was supplied with markers, post-it notes, and big sheets of paper, so while he spoke I was jotting down his main points, like: overwhelmed, alienated, anxious, etc.

We were tasked to be doing something around how we feel about education, so I figured, hey, let's use this thing that's happening right now! He watched me write, and when I asked about his needs, all we had to do was look at the notes. The translations were practically right there!

He was confused and wanting to feel connected. He had that anxiety and behind it a need for ease. We kept going like this for twenty or so minutes. Talking, translating, and writing. He was totally pouring out his heart, his pain. He was needing inclusion, belonging, flexibility, and a sense of ownership.

Really all I did was reflect back the things he said and write them down. Before long, we had in front of us a huge piece of paper with all these words on it.

I said, "Well, we're supposed to be making some kind of a symbol of our ideas here. What do you think about a tree of empathy? I've been sitting here empathizing with you..."

He interjected, "Oh! That's what that is! This has really been helping!"

He seemed to be starting to feel more connected, more relaxed. And he nodded pointing to my notes.

So we put together our empathy tree with all the pain words and needs words written on different post-its. All of these made up the "leaves," some of which were composting at the base of the tree.

Soon time was up, and as we wrapped up the activity, everyone around the room had the opportunity to share. I simply stated this our empathy tree, and that it had grown out of our discussion. But he got up, so animated and eloquent, and went on about how well the experience went.

"Whatever Edwin did for me, it was so great… I was ready to walk out of here! I was so pissed off at all of you folks, but he just really listened!"

The energy in the room changed as he described our process. I could feel a sense of groundedness, of connection as he shared what he did. It seemed everyone was amazed by the open way he spoke.

He kept referring to me and how the change was all about what I did, so people started whispering in my direction, "What did you do? What did you do? What was this magic that you did with him?"

I smiled and said, "I just empathized with him! Seriously, that's it!"

It was like a peak experience for me seeing the power of simple empathy. It was especially noticeable because of the contrast point provided by our facilitator, who kept trying to *explain*, but couldn't hear where we were coming from. Listening makes all the difference sometimes. I really try to remember that.

- Edwin Rutsch, www.cultureofempathy.com

Questioned by the Cops - Christine King

Usually, I don't express my feelings because it seems like a sign of weakness, but recently I was on my way to a party with some of my college friends. We were planning on drinking that night, and I was carrying a container of alcohol from the car into the party house. I wasn't sure if the container was open or not; it was hard to tell based on the way the seal looked.

There were cops at the house when we arrived and, before we got inside, an officer stopped me. He began asking me questions about the container. Since I wasn't sure if it was open or not, and because I knew I was possibly in hot water, I didn't know how to answer him. So I didn't say anything.

The officer asked me for identification but I kept hesitating. He took that as suspicious and I could tell he felt that I was lying to him. When I pulled out my wallet from my back pocket, I told him that I felt nervous and scared because of the vagueness of the rules and explained to him that was why I hesitated to answer.

I thought I was going to be in trouble, but he actually understood my uncertainty. He took pity on me when I told him I was scared. He spent some time going over some information with me about how to handle containers like the one I was holding. He helped me out and we ended up having a nice conversation.

- student excerpt from Christine King's UCSC course "Transformational Communication"

Jack's Funeral - Bridget Belgrave

When I arrived at Jack's funeral I found the large church completely full. Looking around I recognised a lot of people and felt among community. The only space was standing room at the back. I sensed the solemnity among us all as the coffin came in followed by Jack's wife, Marie, and their two young sons.

I find all funeral services intensely moving. The loss, for those close to the person. The utter, irreversible loss. The power of death. The way it is beyond our grip, beyond our understanding. The way it makes visible the huge thing that is every person's life. All this, and the tragic experience of Jack's family, was impacting me in the first moments of the service.

I felt very moved and began to feel a force rising up within me. I did my best to open myself and let the feelings flow. Sometimes this works for me - I can hold myself as the banks of a river while the feeling rushes through - but this time my river banks were dissolving and the huge surge of feeling was fast becoming all that I was. Any moment now it would burst out as a wild, noisy outpouring. We were in England, where the culture for funerals involves weeping, certainly, but not loud shrieking and sobbing! What to do?

I looked towards the door and saw a route I could take which would barely disturb anyone. I'd go outside. That would help. Then, just before moving, I realised how much I wanted to be present, to be part of the service. Something within me resolved to find a way through this, and suddenly I remembered something I had recently learned: with such a strong feeling, there must be an equally strong need underneath it. What could it be?

From nowhere I could identify, an answer came immediately: to worship. I needed to worship. I was surprised. This was not something I would have thought of, and yet I was immediately calmed by this answer. This was it. It felt true. As I focused on my desire to worship, the forceful push of my feeling subsided, like a wave that flows back into the ocean after breaking on the shore. I could feel my feet again. I could stand steady. I could stay in the church. I could worship. I fell into a deep state, totally centred and in sacredness for the rest of the service.

At the end, there was an announcement that family and close friends would proceed to the burial in the cemetery a couple of miles away. I wondered whether I counted as a close friend. Perhaps not, I thought. So I got on my bicycle and pedaled very slowly towards my home - but something stopped me. I didn't feel ready to go home. Instead, I headed to the house of a friend who had also been at the funeral, but she was not there.

I paused, wondering what to do next. Then, even though it was at least ten minutes since the end of the service, without thinking further about it, I began cycling slowly towards the cemetery. I noticed I was still in a deep state, and could hear my inner promptings more clearly than usual, so I decided to trust my impulses for action in each moment. I cycled gently, at the exact speed that felt right to me, enjoying the spring flowers along the roadside in the dappled sunlight.

After about ten minutes I arrived at the large cemetery, park-like and beautiful in the May morning sunshine. I could see the funeral cars quite a distance away, and the mourners with the priest beside the grave. I parked my bike and walked over to join them. Just as I arrived, the burial rituals were completed and the group broke up, embracing each other and talking quietly. I was glad to be there to embrace friends and participate in this moment, but sad to have missed the shared graveside prayers.

Marie and her sons were the first to peel off from the group. They got into the leading funeral car. Others followed their lead and the group dispersed. No longer among the mourners, I wanted a moment to be with Jack, to connect with his spirit.

I went close to the grave and looked down at the coffin, deep in the earth, where his body lay. I picked a few of the daisies that were growing abundantly in the grass and, with a prayer, threw them in. I stood there in silence for some long moments.

While doing this a part of myself was continually feeling alarmed. My mind was telling me I shouldn't do this, it wasn't right, not my place, not respectful. After all, I was not nearly as close to Jack as the others. What would they think? And on and on... But my inner connection was still very strong from my experience in the service, so I managed to stay with my inner promptings.

The last of the family and friends got into their cars and drove off slowly together. I was alone, standing next to Jack's grave. A moment later I felt complete there, but not ready to return to daily life. I saw a bench under a tree some distance away, walked over to it and sat down.

As the last car left the cemetery, I heard a motor start up. A small truck bounced over the grass to the grave. Two men got out and began spading earth onto Jack's coffin. They talked loudly as they worked, joking and chatting. They were full of the vigour of life. They reminded me of the grave diggers in Shakespeare's plays, contrasting life with death, humour with tragedy, lightness with sorrow. In a few efficient and energetic minutes, they had filled the grave and jumped on it to press the earth down, chatting cheerfully all the while. They threw their spades back into the trailer and drove off.

I sat there a while longer in the silence and stillness. It was done.

I did not see Marie during the next days. I had an urge to write to her to say what had happened after she had left the graveyard, but I felt very unsure. To send something so personal at such a sensitive time, would that really be okay? Several days later I felt the urge again and, reconnecting to my decision to follow my inner impulses, I penned her a letter.

Some days later Marie rang me. With her voice full of joy she told me how deeply grateful she was for my letter. She said she had left the graveside to care for her younger son, when he could not take any more. Through the window of the funeral car she had watched me go to the grave, pick the flowers, throw them in, and stand in silent prayer. She told me she had been longing to do exactly this herself, and it was as if I had done it for her. It also meant a lot to her that I had seen the grave filled. It brought her solace and completion.

I was amazed. I had never thought of doing it

for her. Looking back I could see how, from the moment in the church when I became deeply connected with myself, everything had flowed in a "right time, right place, right action" way. It felt like grace, and I felt privileged to have been part of it.

- Bridget Belgrave, www.LifeResources.org.uk

Reframing the Unthinkable - Carol Chase

At the end of teaching a two-hour workshop, a participant, Allison, approached me and said her friend had prompted her to introduce herself to me. This was her second workshop with me on empathy and connection skills, and she wanted to share an experience of hers after hearing one of the other participants ask, "Can we really use this stuff after a couple hours?"

With an earnest face, she told me that this "connection stuff" saved her life.

She didn't give me a lot of details, but did say she'd been robbed while at home with her boyfriend. As one of the thieves held a gun to her head, she found herself thinking, "Wow, I wonder what kind of a childhood this guy must have had to end up here."

She looked him in the eye and felt only compassion. She didn't say anything to him, but was surprised that her thoughts went to such a place in that moment. The robber met her eye contact, then pulled his gun away. Her boyfriend was shot in the foot as the robbers fled, so she knew they were not afraid to use their weapon.

She wanted me to know how appreciative she

was for having been given that insight into caring about another as a human being, no matter what. Allison credited her remembrance of empathy as the tool that saved her life. She wanted me to know that one two-hour workshop could make all the difference in the world. It did to her.

- Carol Chase, revdupcc@juno.com

Left Behind - Jim Manske

I was sitting on my lanai (Hawaiian word for porch) one morning having breakfast, just enjoying some solitude, when I suddenly heard what sounded like a conflict between a mom and a child.

"You come with me right now!" I heard from an adult voice.

I couldn't quite understand what the girl's exact response was, but the tone was definitely, "I don't want to."

As I listened, things got louder. Then, all I could hear was the child's voice screaming over and over again, "Don't leave me, don't leave me, don't leave me!"

Two things happened inside of me. First, I thought about what it was like to be a small, scared child, whose mom apparently just walked away. I thought about how much that girl was needing security, connection, reassurance and so forth.

Second, I went into automatic blame towards the mother. When I noticed this, I took a moment to figure out what was going on with me and realized that I was scared, too. I was worried the little girl might be in danger, but I was also afraid to do anything about it because getting in between a parent and a child is tricky business. I really like to be respectful of parents.

The screaming continued, though, and I couldn't help myself. I followed the sound, motivated by a sense of protection to check things out. When I rounded the corner in my remote, rural neighborhood I saw the girl, who appeared to be no more than four years old, totally freaking out. She was beside herself, and since I was a stranger to her, I approached carefully so I wouldn't scare her more.

I got to be about fifteen feet away from her and I sat down on the ground. I looked at her and she saw me. But she kept staring ahead, yelling "don't leave me, don't leave me."

So, I said to her something like, "Sounds like you're really scared."

She said. "No! I'm not scared!"

I nodded and replied, "Oh, you're really feeling mad."

She said, "Yeah, I'm mad!"

"You wish your mom was here."

She affirmed, "I want my mom to be here. I don't want her to leave me."

I thought this was pretty remarkable for a four-year-old to have such clarity of her needs. That's true of most children at that age; they're very connected to their needs. So I just stayed with her. I said, "Yeah, so you wish your mom was here and you wish she hadn't left you."

She nodded yes, so I said, "It's a little scary for you to be left alone."

And this time, it landed. She softened and said, "Yeah, I'm scared."

Her voice came down and she seemed to be shifting towards calm. Neither of us moved, so I just stayed with her. Soon we began to talk about how she wanted her mom, how she was hungry for breakfast, and about the doll in her clutch.

After a few minutes of chatting, I asked, "Would you like me to take you to your mom?"

She immediately went back into the rage. "NO!"

"Oh, okay." I said. "So you really want your mom to come to you."

She said, "Yeah, yeah." I imagined she was scared that some stranger was going to try to take her somewhere and I didn't blame her at all for that. So we waited and kept connecting.

About that time, Mom showed up. I introduced myself and smiled reassuringly, figuring she was wondering why I was talking to her little girl.

"Sounds like you guys have been having a rough morning."

She sighed in acknowledgement. "Hard day. I haven't been able to get her to do anything I want."

"Yeah," I said, "it's really frustrating when we can't get the kind of cooperation that we think we need."

The mom smiled a little. We kept this empathic dialogue going for a few minutes while I shared about a parenting practice group I co-facilitate and she worked to carve a hole in a coconut for her daughter. She seemed more at ease, more alert, and after a bit she motioned to her daughter to come along so they could go eat more breakfast.

As mom started walking away again, guess what happened? The little girl began to freak out all over again. I said, "Oh, something's going on for you again."

"Yeah..." she replied.

And then the most remarkable thing happened. Mom stepped in and made an empathy guess of her own.

She looked at her daughter and said, "Would you like to lead me the way to the house so we can eat?"

Her little girl took a breath and said, "Yes,

yes."

She held out her hand and took her mom down the driveway without a backwards glance towards me. She was off to breakfast, leading her mom. This is the level of cooperation I love to see between parents and kids.

- Jim Manske, www.radicalcompassion.com

Publishing Your Inspiring Empathy Story

Your Turn! We want your moving "Empathy Story" for future publications! Pinpoint a time that empathy made a difference in an important conversation or relationship. Remind yourself of what happened and how you felt before empathy did its magic. Recount all the details you can "reverse engineer" so the story comes alive, then email it in!

At A Glance:

1. Tell an exciting, heart-warming or relatable story. Your story should be written in the first person and should be about yourself or someone close to you. Especially wanted are stories that take place in work and educational settings.
2. Tell your story in a way that will make the reader cry, laugh, get goosebumps, or say "Wow!"
3. The story should start "in the action" and draw in the reader. Do not start your story with an introduction about what you are going to say, or end with a concluding paragraph about what you just said.

4. Don't try fancy moves with tenses. Writing in the present tense about something that happened in the past rarely works.
5. Keep your story to 1200 words or less. Tighten, tighten, tighten!
6. **Email your completed story to mary@awakenunity.com.**

Guidelines for Submissions

An Empathy Story is an inspirational, true story about ordinary people having moments of extraordinary connection. It is a story that opens the heart and rekindles the spirit. It is a simple piece that touches our readers and helps them discover basic principles they can use in their own lives. These stories are personal and often filled with emotion and drama. They are filled with vivid images created by using the five senses.

Empathy Stories are written in the first person and have a beginning, middle and an end. The stories often close with a punch, creating emotion, rather than simply talking about it. They have heart, but also something extra—an element that makes us all feel more hopeful, more connected, more thankful, more passionate and better about life in general. A good story causes tears, laughter, goose bumps or any combination of these.

Here are some additional questions that may help:

- Did you have to remind yourself to shift from judgment or strategy into empathy?
- Were your empathy skills "clunky" or smooth in the heat of the moment?
- What did you say to yourself in your mind before you spoke out loud?
- Did your feelings seem to shift as a result of the empathy you gave? Did the other person's?
- Did empathy turn a train-wreck of an interaction into something positive?
- Was a closer connection obvious as your story concludes?
- What shape would the story have likely taken if you'd stayed stuck in judgment or blame?
- What are some of the precise words spoken?

What an Empathy Story IS NOT:

- A sermon, an essay or educational piece.
- An opinion about politics or controversial issues.
- An article.

Empathy Practitioners: Biographies

Alan Seid - For more than 25 years, Alan has immersed himself in learning, integrating, and teaching powerful best-practices for personal development and sustainable living. As a seminar leader, facilitator, coach, and special events speaker, his clients have included individuals, couples, and families, as well as organizations and institutions that span the nonprofit, government, business, and academic sectors. Alan is known internationally as a fun, knowledgeable, and engaging presenter, with thousands of online subscribers in over 40 countries and clients in 4 continents. Among his credentials, Alan is a Certified Trainer in Nonviolent Communication. Learn more at: www.cascadiaworkshops.com.

Anne Walton - Anne is a Certified Trainer with the Center for Nonviolent Communication (CNVC). Once she began studying NVC and noticing what a difference it made in her own life, she became passionate about sharing these transformative tools with others. Over the past 11 years, Anne has shared NVC with thousands in Canada, the US and South Korea, at in-person trainings, through teleclasses and on TV. Participants enjoy her authenticity, warmth, clarity and humor. Reach Anne online at www.chooseconnection.com, or by calling 613 204 8824 in Canada or 805 452 5548 in the US.

Becka Kelley - Becka is a Health Psychology Coach at

True North Health Center and a PhD candidate in Psychology at Meridian University. She lectures, leads workshops, and offers private coaching sessions in person, on the phone, and via Skype. Becka works with many individuals in the areas of numbing, emotional eating, and chronic health issues. Becka's passion is supporting people in discovering and aligning themselves with their deepest values. "I believe everyone has the potential and ability to thrive. I am passionate about supporting people in *cultivating connection* and *claiming creativity* in their life and world. I offer listening, reflecting, and the sharing of nourishing practices that support you in living a happy, healthy, and wholehearted life." To set up an appointment please email becka@truenorthhealth.com.

Catherine Cadden - Catherine is a nonviolent activist and educator who squeezes in time for gardening, writing, and playing in the wild. She is the author of Peaceable Revolution Through Education. You can find out more about her work at www.playinthewild.org and www.zenvc.org.

Cedar Rose Selenite - Cedar Rose has been teaching Nonviolent Communication since 2012. She received her training through the Bay Area Nonviolent Communication Yearlong Leadership Program. She studied Empathic Life Coaching with CNVC trainer Francois Beausoleil. Cedar Rose is a Marriage and Family Therapy trainee and volunteers as a counselor at a local agency who serves the gender and sexual minority population part-time. With a lifelong passion for music, she also creates songs for peace and transformation. She helped create the NVC House, an intentional community based on NVC in Chico, CA.

Christine King, MA - Christine has a passion for transformation. For the past six years, she has taught UCSC courses in Transformative Action, Transformation Communication, and Transformative Justice. She also teaches sixth graders communication skills and has spearheaded restorative justice programs at local elementary schools. As a mediator, facilitator, and NVC trainer based out of NVC Santa Cruz, Christine supports groups, individuals, and couples in deepening their communication, compassion, and empathy skills. She also co-developed Grok, a card game designed to develop empathy and relational skills. Learn more and purchase a deck of Grok cards at www.groktheworld.com.

Dian Killian, PhD - Dian is a Certified Trainer with the international Center for Nonviolent Communication, a certified life coach (a graduate of the Coaching for Transformation program) and author of two books, *Urban Empathy: True Life Adventures of Compassion on the Streets of NY*, and *Connecting across Differences: How to Connect with Anyone, Anytime, Anywhere* (now in its third edition, and in German). Founder and former director of the Center for

Collaborative Communication, she now offers coaching and training via her company, Work Collaboratively, to diverse organizations from small and large NGOs to multinational and Fortune 100 companies. She also leads the annual NVC East Coast Women's Retreat and has regularly offered public programming at Kripalu, the 92nd St Y, Omega, the NY Open Center, NVC Academy, and in the Bahamas and Europe. Learn more and join her blog post and mailing list at www.workcollaboratively.com.

Edwin Rutsch - Edwin is director of the Center for Building a Culture of Empathy, which is the internet's largest resource site for empathy-related resources. Edwin is also founder of the International Empathy Trainers Association. Learn more at www.cultureofempathy.com.

Hemlata Pokharna - Hema Pokharna, PhD, is a scientist, writer, speaker and Nonviolent Communication certified trainer with more than 20 years of experience coaching clients toward wholeness, collaborative communication, and resilient leadership. Hema is also an interfaith peacemaker and mediator, and has served on the board of Parliament of World Religions. Together with her physician sister, Mandakini, also an NVC certified trainer, Hemlata inspires and educates people around the world to make healthy, harmonious life choices.

Jean Morrison, MA - Jean has been providing trainings, consultation, and mediation for diverse groups and organizations for the past 23 years. Jean's work integrates whole brain learning and thinking, experiential learning and interactive games, lifestyle management, and the Enneagram system of personality studies. She has been a certified trainer with the international Center for Nonviolent Communication (NVC) since 1989. She co-founded NVC Santa Cruz and she is currently creating materials to support compassionate communication around the world. Learn more atwww.groktheworld.com.

Jim and Jori Manske - For more than 37 years, Jim and Jori Manske have partnered both in life and work. As co-creators of Peaceworks, they offer training, mediation, facilitation, organizational development, consulting, and mentoring. They are both Certified Trainers for and have been leaders in the international Center for Nonviolent Communication. For the past two years, they have supported the transformation of that organization through the New Future Process. They co-authored *Pathways to Liberation* along with two colleagues, a self-assessment tool used globally by those seeking to become certified trainers. Currently living in Haiku, Maui, Jim and Jori contribute to Hawaii NVC and the Network for Nonviolent Communication. They offer weekly practice groups in Maui and via teleconference, and enjoy contributing to the growing

NVC communities of Asia.

Katherine Revoir - Her role as a counselor is to provide you with tools that heal, comfort, and encourage you to access and follow your own inner guidance. Her clients experience more emotional balance, peace, clear thinking, and choice. These changes can happen with remarkable ease. She practices the tools of Interpersonal Neurobiology, and brings over 25 years of training and experience as a mentor and spiritual counselor. In your work together, you can integrate your physical, emotional, and spiritual needs, so that you live with more joy, clarity, and freedom. She'd love to support you in making your life more wonderful. Contact her at www.RicherLiving.org/Counseling.

LaShelle Lowe-Charde - LaShelle has been certified as a trainer in Compassionate Communication (NVC) for ten years. She holds a master's degree in psychology and has worked as a trainer for the past 15 years. She brings a deep relationship to mindfulness practice that she has cultivated through many years of Zen practice and training in Hakomi (Mindfulness Based Therapy).

Mair Alight - Mair has dedicated much of her life to service, striving to live in alignment with her values; clear communication, sharing empathy key skills and practicing self-responsibility in the service of Life. Mair is a Certified Trainer with the Center for Nonviolent

Communication. Since 2000, Mair has been learning and sharing Nonviolent Communication (from prisoners to pre-schoolers) with group and individual coaching and training calls, and in-person teaching, sharing and practice on the farm and elsewhere. Mair spent 500+ hours learning from Marshall Rosenberg, developer of NVC. She is a volunteer with the Seattle Freedom Project. Mair is an Empathy Specialist, and has set up PHEW! a Free Empathy Warmline (not a crisis hotline). Mair has taken her love of NVC practice to Canada, England, Ethiopia, Mexico and Switzerland. Mair is thrilled to have opened a Zazzle store combining her love of beauty, art, and communication. This year she published *Vashon-Maury Island Coloring Book*, and is working on *Tools, Not Rules: Handbook for a Living Language*. She has published a children's coloring book *Compassionate Underwear* and co-produced a DVD "Living NVC". Learn more at Mair@MairAlight.com.

Mary Goyer - Mary Goyer, M.S., is a holistic counselor & trainer specializing in the intersection of leadership development, connection skills, and personal development for executives in high-impact organizations. She draws upon her traditional training in Marriage & Family Therapy (MFT), her background in conscious communication, and her expertise in mind-body healing techniques to help professionals in struggling teams tap into their creative, collaborative potential, and to move forward in a satisfying career. Mary's warm, interdisciplinary approach for busy professionals combines her training, coaching, and counseling backgrounds to support the individuals in organizations who are good at what they do, but are not so skilled at leading and managing. She helps them cultivate the relationship skills that make a true impact – at work, at home, and in the larger community. Learn more at www.consciouscommunication.co.

Miki Kashtan - Miki is a co-founder of Bay Area Nonviolent Communication (BayNVC) and Lead Collaboration Consultant at the Center for Efficient Collaboration. She aims to support visionary leadership and shape a livable future using collaborative tools based on the principles of Nonviolent Communication. She shares these tools through meeting facilitation, mediation, consulting, coaching, and training for organizations and committed individuals. Her latest book, *Reweaving Our Human Fabric: Working together to Create a Nonviolent Future* (2015) explores the practices and systems needed for a collaborative, empathic society and includes fictional stories set in a future such society. She is also the author of *Spinning Threads of Radical Aliveness: Transcending the Legacy of Separation in Our Individual Lives*, and *The Little Book of Courageous Living*. Miki blogs at *The Fearless Heart* and her articles have appeared in the *New York Times* (*"Want Teamwork? Encourage Free Speech"*), Tikkun, Waging Nonviolence, Shareable, Peace and Conflict, and elsewhere. She holds a Ph.D. in Sociology from UC Berkeley. Learn more at www.thefearlessheart.org.

Sarah Peyton - Sarah is a certified trainer of Nonviolent Communication and is the author of the book "Your Resonant Self: Guided meditations and exercises to engage your brain's capacity for healing," coming out from Norton Publishing in September of 2017.

Thom Bond - Thom brings 29 years of human potential experience and training experience to his work as an Internationally Certified NVC Trainer. His passion and knowledge of Nonviolent Communication (NVC) combine to create a practical, understandable, humorous, and potentially profound approach for learning and integrating the skills of peacemaking. He is described as concise, inspiring, sincere and optimistic, applying transformational and spiritual ideas and sensibilities to real-life situations. Many of his students become active facilitators, trainers, and practitioners. As a trainer, speaker, mediator, and coach, Thom has taught tens of thousands of clients, participants, readers and listeners Nonviolent Communication. He has been published or featured in The New York Times, New York Magazine, and Yoga Magazine. He is a founder and the Director of Education for The New York Center for Nonviolent Communication, the creator of The Compassion Course, a member of the Communications Coordination Committee for the United Nations and a CNVC IIT trainer. Learn more about his work at www.nycnvc.org or join next year's online NVC based Compassion Course at www.compassioncourse.org.

Timothy Regan - Timothy is a born-and-raised San Franciscan who is committed to the restoration of empathy as a cultural skill everywhere people communicate. He has been practicing mind-body healing with individuals and groups as a healthy lifestyle counselor at Kaiser Permanente for 18 years. He is also licensed in California as a Clinical Social Worker, and he has an independent practice of offering training in conscious and effective communication, mediation, healing relationships between people, and creating peace within one's self. Timothy loves working with people from all traditions and cultures, who are seeking a better way of being with each other and collaborating in the challenging work of our time (the protection and regeneration of all life and the resources that give life). He is a Certification Candidate with the Center for Nonviolent Communication and can be reached at admin@rememberingconnection.com.

Victoria Kindle Hodson - Victoria Kindle Hodson, consultant, trainer, teacher, and internationally recognized author, is a passionate proponent of respectful interaction between adults and young people. For four decades, she has been sharing compassionate practices from the fields of parenting, education, positive psychology, and brain science with tens of thousands of parents, teachers, and students. As well as developing *The No-Fault Zone Game*, a hands-on communication and conflict resolution tool that is being used widely in homes and classrooms throughout the world, in partnership with Sura Hart, Victoria has written three books based on Nonviolent Communication^{SM} that have been translated into numerous languages: *Respectful Parents, Respectful Kids, The Compassionate Classroom, and The No-Fault Classroom.* Victoria lives in Ventura, California and is currently developing personalized learning and social-emotional skill development programs for schools. Learn more at www.thenofaultzone.com.

Appendix A: "Not Empathy" Quick Reference Sheet

	Instead of This...	Try That...	
Educating	"He's just doing his best. It's hard for people who grew up in his situation to not get defensive hearing feedback."	*Keep your focus on what they're saying until they request your opinion.*	"So it's painful and unproductive to talk with him when he's that upset. Hard."
Advice	"You know, I read that 70-85% of fertility issues can be shifted with nutritional changes. You should try that."	*Recognize your desire to help/fix, but stay with them in their unfolding story.*	"Wow, so you're wondering if there's really anything you can do for your body."
Reassurance	"I think you did a good job at the pitch. Don't worry, you're doing fine on the new team."	*Guess a feeling that might be up for them.*	"Is it that you're worried about your job or just that you felt vulnerable today?"
Coaching	"I want to invite you to take a breath right now..."	*Wait till they ask for suggestions.*	"Sounds like things seem crazy overwhelming right now!"

Sympathy	"I hate it when that happens! I'm so pissed! You don't deserve that."	*Note to yourself how their story triggers you, but keep the spotlight on them.*	**"You're furious about the email she sent! You all had worked hard and decided on a plan already!"**
Spiritualizing	"These things always happen for a reason."	*Guess what they might be needing and see if it resonates.*	**"Yeah, so you're just needing some sign it's going to work itself out? Hope?"**
Colluding (Agreeing/ Disagreeing)	"You're right about him being irresponsible. He's so immature."	*Reflect what you're hearing without agreeing it's the gospel truth.*	**"So part of you is concerned he's not going to come through. Ugh."**
Evaluating	"I think it's good that you told your kids what's going on. It's healthy for them to know!"	*Trust they'll find their own truth, organically, without your directing the process.*	**"You're second-guessing how you presented this to the kids? But you wanted to be honest as possible?"**
Story Telling	"I know what you mean! That's exactly what my wife does, too. She always manages to…."	*Keep it about them until they're done. Then share if they have space to listen.*	**"So she was upset and you ended up feeling guilty? Even though you'd warned her about the traffic?"**

184

Appendix B: Planned Empathy Practice

Usually, we think of empathy as something we offer off the cuff when someone's upset. It's a spur of the moment thing, to weave a little empathy into some dialogue with a sad lover, an angry stranger, or what have you. It is also, however, a great idea to *plan* empathy if there's someone in your life who is game to give it a try in a more formal, deliberate way. This is, in fact, one of the best strategies I know of to practice changing those "NOT EMPATHY" defaults and to experiment with new, empathic connections.

Empathy, as it's presented in this book, is counter-cultural and feels a little unnatural for most people. So changing the way you think and talk – when you simply want to help someone who's down – takes some effort and mindfulness. In fact, if you ever study NVC in any kind of longer-term program, you might even be assigned an "empathy buddy" to practice with weekly. But it's something you can create for yourself, and all you need is a willing partner and a phone.

Here's the idea of an empathy buddy: Set aside time to talk on the phone (or on Skype) for 20-60 minutes in total. You'll spend half that time being listened to as you share whatever's up for you in that moment, good or bad, happy or sad. You can share anything. While your partner tries to listen empathically, notice how it feels to be heard in this way, how well it works or doesn't work for you.

But when it's your turn to be the listener to whatever's going on in your buddy's life, try to practice *not* giving them advice, *not* reassuring them, etc. Instead, begin by focusing on three basic skills:

1. Reflecting back, or **recapping**, the gist of what they're saying (not an easy task when they're upset and all over the place).

2. Guessing the **feelings** most up for them (print this copy of the feelings list to help you out).

3. Guessing the **needs** connected to those feelings (print this copy of the needs list to reference) that seem to be in the mix.

It's not exactly a linear process, and can definitely feel a tad – or a ton – mechanical during the earlier attempts. But still, it is a good, concrete place to start.

To further get things going, I've worked up a checklist of sorts to support you during any *planned exchanges* where you want to practice offering empathy. If it feels helpful, use the checklist to track which micro-skills were accessible for you during a given practice session as the empathy "giver" or "receiver."

Remember though, every conversation will call for different skills; the goal is *not* about checking off all the boxes. The goal, rather simply, is for the empathy receiver to feel more understood and self-connected, which might be accomplished with as little as five minutes of warm, quiet listening from the giver. It all depends! In other words, this tool is intended to support mindfulness, not create a rigid prescription.

The Empathy "Giver" (the listener)
- I showed up with a warm presence
- I offered a recap
- I offered a feelings or a needs guess
- I asked about body sensations
- I offered one digestible guess at a time
- I tried to let the Receiver's rhythm determine the pace of my guesses
- I felt comfortable hearing that a guess didn't resonate
- I noticed when I felt compelled to mention a strategy or advice
- I let my partner know if I was "full" or triggered
- I wrapped up at the agreed upon time

The Empathy "Receiver" (the speaker)
- I made a request for a recap
- I made a request for a feelings or needs guess
- I felt comfortable saying that a guess didn't resonate
- I paused every so often to allow the Giver a chance to speak and make their guesses
- I connected more deeply with my feelings during this session
- I connected more deeply with my needs during this session
- I connected more to my body sensations during this session
- A new idea, possibility, and/or strategy popped up organically during this session
- I felt comfortable wrapping up a topic thread when I was complete

Debrief

- What worked well for me during this session was _____.
- What I noticed about myself in each role was _____.
- Next time, I'm hopeful that _____.

What you can experiment with, if you like, is having the checklist in front of you to reference *before or after* empathy each time you talk with your buddy. You may:

Intend to focus on a specific micro-skill. (Example: I'm going to try today to make shorter empathy guesses, and talk in shorter "segments" when I'm the receiver.)

Intend to notice progress over time. (Example: Wow, making a needs guess is practically second nature these days! I don't even have to think about it like I used to!)

Watch for trends. (Example: Hmm, I often check off the same items, but have not so far tuned into body sensations. Interesting - is that because I don't notice my body sensations at all during empathy or I just haven't brought it up verbally?)

What if you don't know anyone who wants to be an empathy buddy, but you'd really like to practice? Here are a few suggestions:

- Tap into the network of a local NVC trainer or community for recommendations.

- Search for and join NVC-related Yahoo or Google groups online, or join one of the many NVC groups on Facebook. Start a thread asking for suggestions. In some groups, it's normal to get empathy in writing straight from your post!

- Practice *silently* translating the complaints and judgments from your loved ones into feelings and needs. Just make the guess in your head without verbalizing anything.

- Practice translating your own complaints and judgments into feelings and needs.

- Consider getting someone's okay before offering formal empathy guesses. If you let them know ahead of time that you're going to try something you recently learned, they likely won't be off-put by your languaging. "Are you feeling X because you're needing Y?" isn't exactly a normal thing for most of us to hear.

Appendix C: Special Notes for Newbies

If you're excited to go out there and empathize your heart out, I've done my job. Still there are a few things that often come up for newbies. I want to offer a few tips to make your learning curve a little more gentle.

If this comes up...	Remember...	It might sound like this...
You're attached to your empathy guesses being right and it's hard to hear that a guess is off... *You: Was some part of you scared in that moment?* *Them: No, not really.* *You: Oh... are you sure you weren't a little worried?*	It's normal to want to be right. And it feels damn good to be helpful! You'll never tire of the little rush that comes when you hear, "Yes, that's it! Thank you!!" Perhaps it has something to do with competence, mattering, and contributing! However, it can also be incredibly valuable for people to clarify all that's *not* contributing to their distress. Narrowing things down can really be a gift, especially when someone is navigating something that feels vague or amorphous to them.	*You: Was some part of you scared in that moment?* *Them: No, not really.* *You: Ok, so fear isn't quite it.* *Them: It's actually a relief to know fear isn't part of this; anxiety used to be such a biggie for me.* *You: So a tiny celebration that fear isn't in the mix?* *Them: Yeah, totally. I think it's more about boundaries and determination, now.*

If this comes up...	Remember...	It might sound like this...
You're hesitant to make a guess unless you're pretty sure it's "right." Or your mind goes blank from performance anxiety... *Them: ...So, anyway, I don't know what to think! Do you have any "needs" guesses for me?* *You: Umm. You already said you're mad. So anger. Umm... I don't know.*	Self-consciousness is so, so normal, especially when you're learning something new that you really care about. But it's hard to be present when your self-consciousness is in the driver's seat Bring your attention back to their words, take a breath, and let it be enough to bring warm attunement to what they're saying.	*Them: ...So, anyway, I don't know what to think. Do you have any "needs" guesses for me?* *You: Hmm. (deep breath.) You mentioned anger, but a "needs" guess? ...Can I recap the main things I heard, first, just to make sure I got the gist of everything? That might help me get clearer.* *Them: Sure!*
They begin to explain why your empathy guess didn't land for them, but as they do, it sounds like they just didn't understand. *You: Were you needing integration?* *Them: No. I just wanted these parts to come together better. I wanted more union.* *You: That's what I meant about integration.*	It happens! Resist the urge to educate or explain why you guessed what you did. Let them pick the verbiage that works for them and go with it. The key is that you understand what they're trying to convey, and that they're feeling heard!	*You: Were you needing integration?* *Them: No. I just wanted these parts to come together better. I wanted more union.* *You: Okay, so "union" is what clicks, huh? Got it.*

191

If this comes up...	Remember...	It might sound like this...
You think you should've done more or said more. You think you didn't help enough. *You: Was this about consideration?* *Them: I guess so. And now that I think about it, consideration actually comes down to reassurance. I'm just wanting some peace in this relationship! I want to trust it without question!!*	Some people just need a tiny nudge in order to begin talking themselves all the way through their own process: guessing their own feelings and needs, coming up with spontaneous ah-has, etc. Remember, if they feel understood and more in touch with themselves at the end of a conversation, it's a win!	*You: Was this about consideration?* *Them: I guess so. And now that I think about it, consideration actually comes down to reassurance. I'm just wanting some peace in this relationship! I want to trust it without question!!* *You: Wow, good to be in touch with all that?*
You feel mechanical in the way you're making guesses. *Them: I've just been feeling so devastated by this loss. I can't even begin to say.* *You: Are you feeling sad because you need connection?*	It's normal to feel awkward when trying to connect in this new, counter-cultural way of listening, which involves a lot of un-learning. Be gentle with yourself as you practice new skills while expressing your care. (Seek out some empathy experts in your area. You'll pick up a lot about "naturalizing" empathy just by listening to them speak during their trainings, etc.)	*Them: I've just been feeling so devastated by this loss. I can't even begin to say.* *You: Ugh, (nodding) just so sad.* *Them: Yeah (tearing up).* *You: (audible breath) Yeah. Really missing that connection.* *Them: Yes! I don't have anyone right now!*

If this comes up...	Remember...	It might sound like this...
The other person doesn't seem to be enjoying the empathy you're offering. Somehow it doesn't seem to be clicking.	It might not be working for them, and there could be any number of reasons as to why, which may or may not have anything to do with you. Be willing to let empathy go if, after a bit of a try, it's still not clicking. See if you can sense into what'd be more connective.	*You: Is this feeling helpful, me just listening like this? Or are you wanting something different?* *Them: Well, I guess I'd like to know if you've ever been in my shoes. Has this ever happened to you?* *You: Totally! I can tell you my story if you'd like.*
People think you're talking weird and it makes them uncomfortable. *Them: Why are you talking like that, anyway?* *You: You're confused and wanting clarity?* *Them: Stop it!*	Focusing on feelings and needs will sound strange to people at times. They may worry they're being judged, taken advantage of, or "handled" in some way. Be transparent: this is something you're trying for the sake of connection. And if they ask about your language, it's an indication that, perhaps, they're feeling less connected rather than more. So adjust accordingly and see how it goes.	*Them: Why are you talking like that?* *You: Oh! Right. I guess I'm trying something from a book I read, but I'm a beginner. Is it a little off-putting?* *Them: Yeah, a little!* *You: Sorry. Just trying to be present, actually. I really do care about what you were saying. Up to going back to where you left off?*

If this comes up…	Remember…	It might sound like this…
You start feeling annoyed by all the times you're NOT met with empathy when it's your turn to be listened to. *You: So it's all been a lot to sort through.* *Them: Why don't you try and set it up with a calendar app?* *You: Oh, yeah, I have one already. I just can't seem to get myself to follow through.* *Them: What about trying…* *You: This isn't empathy!*	It can be #@%&ing annoying to get one "empathy-not" after another when it's your turn to be heard. You so want the relief and internal settling that comes with being held in your process, but you can only coach a listener so much. A quick request for "just listening" might help, but if not, here are a few more ideas: Seek out some resources on self-empathy; Find an empathy buddy – someone who, like you, wants to learn how to listen empathically; Plug into an online NVC hub and get some empathy there; Offer an NVC book to your listener (if you sense they'd welcome that suggestion). I do not recommend trying to "reform" all the listeners in your life into proper empathizers, or else you'll *all* be annoyed.	*You: So it's all been a lot to sort through.* *Them: Why don't you try and set it up with a calendar app?* *You: Oh, yeah, I have one already. I just can't seem to get myself to follow through.* *Them: What about trying…* *You: Let me just stop you for a sec. Right now, I'm not ready for ideas. Do you have space just to listen a bit?* *Them: Sure, it's just that…* *You, mentally switching into self-empathy: [I'm so wanting space to be heard. And I'm overwhelmed and frustrated that this feels so hard right now.]*

About the Editor

 **Mary Goyer, M.S.**, is a holistic counselor & trainer specializing in the intersection of leadership development, connection skills, and personal development for executives in high-impact organizations. She draws upon her traditional training in Marriage & Family Therapy (MFT), her background in conscious communication, and her expertise in mind-body healing techniques to help professionals in struggling teams tap into their creative, collaborative potential, and to move forward in a satisfying career.

Mary spent the first part of her career as an educator, counselor, and consultant working with "at-risk" tweens and teens. She supported students directly for years, and continues to offer her work in schools, providing keynotes and training for educators. Her passion for teaching intra/interpersonal skills is part of Mary's holistic approach to encourage students' academic success, ultimately helping them grow into contributing, balanced adults. This passion has inspired numerous corporate/school partnership projects which aim to resource schools with social-emotional programming for their students, teachers, and parents.

Mary's warm, interdisciplinary approach for busy professionals combines her training, coaching, and counseling backgrounds to support the individuals in organizations who are good at what they do, but are not so skilled at leading and managing. She helps them cultivate the relationship skills that make a true impact—at work, at home, and in the larger community. Find out more at www.consciouscommunication.co.